THE ROYAL HORTICULTURAL SOCIETY
PRACTICAL GUIDES

PATIOS AND COURTYARDS

THE ROYAL HORTICULTURAL SOCIETY
PRACTICAL GUIDES

PATIOS AND COURTYARDS

Tim Newbury

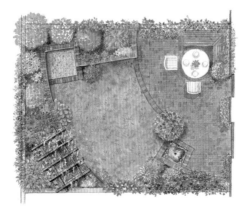

A Dorling Kindersley Book

DK

LONDON, NEW YORK, MUNICH,
MELBOURNE, DELHI

PROJECT EDITOR Lin Hawthorne
ART EDITOR Martin Hendry

SERIES EDITOR Annelise Evans
SERIES ART EDITOR Ursula Dawson

MANAGING EDITOR Anna Kruger
MANAGING ART EDITOR Lee Griffiths

DTP DESIGNERS Louise Paddick, Louise Waller

PRODUCTION MANAGER Sarah Coltman

First published in Great Britain in 2001
Reprinted 2002
by Dorling Kindersley Limited
80 Strand, London WC2R 0RL

A Penguin Company

A CIP catalogue for this book is available from the British Library.
ISBN 0 7513 47116

Reproduced by Colourscan, Singapore
Printed and bound by Star Standard Industries PTE Ltd, Singapore

see our complete
catalogue at

www.dk.com

CONTENTS

DESIGNING PATIOS AND COURTYARDS

AN OUTDOOR ROOM

THE CONCEPT OF A GARDEN as an extension of the home is by no means new, but as the demands of modern life encroach on space and time, the idea of spilling out into the garden at the drop of a hat has renewed appeal. There is something deeply refreshing about sitting out in the open air, sheltered by lush greenery, listening to the splash of moving water, catching the sun and soaking up the ambience as you sip on a cool drink and enjoy the view.

PATIOS AND COURTYARDS

Historically, the term "patio" was applied to an inner courtyard such as those that typify the old Moorish gardens of Spain. Over the years, however, the terms patio and courtyard have acquired separate identities. Essentially, a courtyard is a space that is enclosed on all sides and open to the sky. Within the space, plants and ornament

> In most climates, outdoor rooms need some shelter from the elements

may be used in myriad styles to exploit the differing aspects of the enclosing walls and typically sheltered microclimate.

A patio is nearly always a paved area next to the house – often linked to it by means of a French window or sliding door. It is generally not enclosed and is often best sited in a sheltered but unrestricted position that makes the most of the sun or, in hot climates, ensures shade from burning rays.

ANCIENT INSPIRATION
This peaceful and cloistered Spanish courtyard inspires quiet and gentle contemplation – a perfect model for the modern equivalent that seeks to provide respite from the rat race.

◀ THE BEST OF BOTH WORLDS *A patio thoughtfully designed can offer both sun and shade.*

CREATING A WISH LIST

WHETHER YOU ARE ABOUT TO embark on designing a complete garden, as in a courtyard, or just part of one, as in a patio, the starting point for your design is always to ask "What exactly do I want?". The answer will invariably comprise several items, and these will form the bones of your wish list. Some address practicalities, such as having space for a table and chairs, while others will be more personal, like needing a display area for your collection of Bonsai.

IDENTIFYING YOUR NEEDS

The success of a design depends on it meeting the needs of all who use it and on considering how it will be used. A family garden almost invariably needs safe play space, for example, while households with gardeners of limited mobility might wish to build in raised beds to make gardening easier. Where dining and entertaining are priorities, a carefully planned patio can take this outdoors in unrestricted comfort.

You should bear in mind the time you wish to spend looking after your patio or courtyard. If time is short, avoid massed annual bedding, or plants that require intensive trimming, pruning or tying in.

It is helpful to organize your wish list in order of priority, with the least important – and most expendable items – at the bottom.

Safety is paramount in any garden, especially where children are present, and must be considered at the planning stage. Use safe water features such as bubble fountains and make sure that any chosen paving materials are not slippery when wet. Check that any plants are not toxic, or otherwise dangerous because of large thorns, for example. Outdoor electricity supplies should be low-voltage, or protected by an earth leakage device (circuit breaker). Installing mains electricity outdoors is a job for the professionals.

FAMILY AREA
An elegant solution is often possible, as shown here, where small children share the garden with parents who are committed gardeners. The sand pit forms part of a play area that allows for safe supervision from the relative comfort of a bench surrounded by durable and fragrant climbers and plants in sturdy, stable pots.

◀ NIGHT AND DAY
This subtle lighting not only extends the potential for patio use in the evenings, it also adds a charming ambience from which to admire the views.

▼ SOME LIKE IT HOT
A hot tub is a costly item but may be high on the wish list of the committed hedonist. It demands practical consideration of surrounding paving textures, however, if it is to remain safe even when wet.

TAKE CARE OF THE PENNIES

If you try, as far as possible, to cost each item on your wish list, when you begin to design, you can incorporate each vital item up to the point where you have filled the available space without over-stretching your budget. The cost of work is a major consideration, and you can find that the immediately available budget is gobbled up by the first item on your list. If so, phase

> Phasing a project can be an economic means to an ideal end

your project over a period, so that you can spread costs but still achieve the ideal end. With a patio, this could mean laying flags in phase one, perhaps with a few shrubs or trees as a framework. Phase two might add a water feature and some infill shrubs, with the final phase completing the picture with pretty perennials and grasses and finishing touches, such as a sundial or statue.

SUITING YOUR LIFESTYLE

• If you are a social animal, make sure that paved areas are big enough to accommodate your guests around an outdoor dining table.
• If you cook and dine outdoors regularly, consider installing a built-in barbecue and garden lighting for night-time use.
• If you enjoy gardening, be sure to build in areas for storage of tools and equipment.
• If your garden is overlooked, consider using a pergola or trellis work to provide some screening for more privacy.

ASSESSING YOUR SITE

WITH YOUR WISH LIST IN MIND, the next stage in the design process is to assess your plot and take stock of what is there – if anything! The aim is to decide which features are to stay – though possibly in need of renovation or improvement – and which must go. It is tempting, especially if you inherit an old, neglected garden, to clear the decks and start afresh. This may indeed be the best solution, but beware of discarding hidden gems.

TAKING STOCK

Be quite strict with yourself when taking stock– any features that you choose to retain must have a definite purpose and form an integral part of the final design. There is no sense in, say, retaining an existing pool, if it happens to occupy the only sunny part of the garden where you would ideally like to place your patio.

Some elements must be kept, because either the cost of removing them would be prohibitive, for example, a large, brick outbuilding, or else they are essential, such as a cover for an inspection chamber. In these situations, you might choose to

OUT WITH THE OLD?

• Before grubbing out trees and large shrubs, give them a thorough health check and, if necessary, research how they respond to renovation pruning. If retained, they will provide an air of maturity that new, young plants may not attain for years.

• Bear in mind that the cost of removal of large plants, or old paving and brickwork, may be substantial and could seriously eat into your gardening budget.

LIVING SCULPTURES
Many trees become increasingly picturesque with age, here forming a valuable focal point. The effect would take years to recreate.

disguise the objects in question, perhaps by screening them from view with trellis and plants. Inspection covers can be enclosed by spreading plants, or you can buy specially recessed covers into which flags or pavers can be set, thereby merging them almost seamlessly with surrounding paving. Alternatively, with a little imagination, you can convert problem areas into positive design features. You might, for example, consider painting the doors and windows of an outbuilding and treating the walls to a colour wash, choosing a colour that forms a unifying element in the overall scheme.

CONSIDER THE PRACTICALITIES

Linking house and garden is important to a successful design and you should look at the various options open for you to do this. If you intend to use your patio for *al fresco* dining at every opportunity for example, locate it with easy access in mind, near the kitchen or dining-room door. Water and electricity may figure in your plans, so take a look at how existing taps and power

points fit into the scheme of things. If their placement is inconvenient, you can consider how you will resite them.

Assess your own capabilities and the time available to carry out the various tasks. Then balance this against the extra cost and convenience of using professional help for specialized jobs, like bricklaying and especially electrical work, for which safety must be given the highest priority.

▲ USEFUL SEATING
A storage box for toys, tools, or fold-away patio furniture can be cleverly disguised as an attractive and functional seat.

◄ MAKE IT A VIRTUE
Every household has its share of visually unappealing, but necessary, objects. Here, garden tools and dustbins are imaginatively hidden by a feature that makes a pretty cameo in its own right.

MAKING THE BEST OF IT

If you inherit a flat area of concrete, but cannot afford to rip it up, do not despair. Existing concrete can be paved over directly with flags, or brick pavers, if levels allow, or you could improve the look immensely by applying a layer of gravel or stone chippings. An empty expanse is a visual bore, but concrete makes perfect hard standing for arrangements of planted containers and ornaments, such as statuary. You might introduce further interest with small raised beds. Provided that they drain freely from the base, simple raised beds can be made from heavy timbers, such as railway sleepers, laid directly on concrete.

While most gardens are fairly flat, a great many slope quite steeply. If a level area for a patio is high on your wish list, work will clearly need to be done to modify the slope accordingly. This involves terracing, with retaining walls to allow you to cut into the slope far enough to achieve the desired space. The steeper the slope, the greater the weight of soil the walls will need to retain and, in many regions, the specifications are subject to local building regulations.

In this case, unless you are a skilled and experienced builder, you would be well advised to call in professionals to guarantee a safe and structurally sound outcome.

SOME THINGS NEVER CHANGE...

Many of the physical structures in your plot are more or less amenable to change. But some courtyard gardens will always have areas that are dark and shady due to

> ### Lift dark and shady areas by painting walls in pale colours or vibrant hues

lack of direct sunlight. Such areas can be lifted by using pale-coloured paving and by painting surrounding walls in light colours, or in really bright and vibrant hues.

Other constants include the climate and light and moisture levels on site. Observe your garden throughout the year and you will gradually discover the hottest and coolest places, and any that are dry or damp. You will also notice places that are

TO THE FORE
A collection of planted containers of varying shapes and sizes can transform a boring expanse of paving almost instantly. Interest can easily be sustained by bringing container plants to front of stage just as they reach the peak of perfection.

▲ A SHADY COURTYARD
Shade-loving plants provide a lush framework to this intimate space and light-hungry ones in pots occupy every available pool of sunlight.

more sheltered or draughty than others. Each of these conditions has great potential for adding interest and quality to your design if viewed positively. There will be certain items on your wish list that are more suited to one condition than another, so careful site selection is essential.

A patio in cool climates, for example, is best in a sunny, sheltered site, whereas in hotter regions, you may want at least one paved area in shade, preferably in the path of cooling breezes.

Planting is the ultimate key to success in a design. With a little research, you will find plants to suit any soil and situation, from heavy clay in shade, to sandy soils in full sun. Adopt the principle of choosing the plants to suit the conditions, rather than changing conditions to suit the plants and they will have every chance of thriving.

SUNTRAP PATIO
This patio is sited at a distance from the house to make the most of the day's sun. Notice that the area beside the house is in deep shade even on this bright summer day.

A SPECIAL MICROCLIMATE

A MICROCLIMATE IS, IN SIMPLE TERMS, a climate found in a restricted area. Cities, for example, are slightly warmer, on average, than open country, due to the "radiator effect" of the brick, concrete, and asphalt found in them. At the garden level, microclimate describes variations in climate found within a garden. By and large, courtyards and patios have a very special microclimate, simply by virtue of what they are – to be used to advantage by people and plants alike.

HOT SPOTS

Patios usually lie in close proximity to a building and are likely to be in sun for a substantial part of the day. They may also be protected from wind, perhaps by trellis or large shrubs. As a result, a patio area is warmer and more sheltered than a more open part of the garden, making it far more attractive and comfortable, especially at either end of the day.

During the day, paving and sunny walls both reflect and absorb the sun's heat. The gradual release of heat in the evening, when the sun has disappeared is, in effect, a sort

◀ SUN TRAP
Screened from wind and sheltered from prying eyes by tall shrubs, this patio has been carefully sited to gain the full benefits of the day's sun.

▼ SUN-LOVERS
Succulent, rosette-forming plants, like this houseleek, Sempervivum montanum, *are perfectly adapted to dry heat and will thrive in a hot spot.*

PLANTS FOR A HOT SPOT

Achillea millefolium 'Moonshine' Perennial with finely divided, grey-green leaves and flat heads of many tiny yellow flowers all summer.
Osteospermum ecklonis Perennial with grey-green leaves and white, daisy-like flowers, indigo-blue on the reverse, all summer.
Lavandula angustifolia, Lavender Aromatic, grey-leaved, shrubby evergreen with spikes of pale to deep purple flowers in summer.
Salvia officinalis, Sage Shrubby evergreen with aromatic, grey-green leaves and spikes of blue-purple flowers in summer.

of storage radiator. This allows plants that might not do well in a colder, more exposed position in the garden to thrive and extends their growing season by warming the soil earlier and later in the year. It also means that a patio is comfortably warm for an extended period on the cooler days of autumn and spring.

ENCLOSED AREAS

Courtyards are usually enclosed on all sides by walls and, depending on their height, they may experience a whole range of lighting conditions from full sun through to deep shade. As well as determining areas of sun and shade, walls also provide shelter from the cooling effects of prevailing winds. As a result, it can be several degrees warmer inside a courtyard than outside it on a windy day. This has benefits aside from comfort. The relative lack of air movement, combined with the enhanced humidity provided by plants, damp soil, and perhaps water in a pool or fountain, intensifies the fragrance of scented plants and allows it to permeate over a wide area. If you do choose to include the

humidity-enhancing virtues of a tinkling fountain, you will find that the sound is amplified in a most pleasing way by the echoes from the surrounding walls.

Sunny walls and paving within a courtyard confer the same benefits in terms of warmth, shelter, and comfort as does a

Within a space of a few metres, you can enjoy hot sun or cool shade

patio. For every sunny courtyard wall, however, there will one facing the opposite direction that is in shadow. So within the space of a few metres, you can move from a hot, sunny position to one in cool shade. This transition allows you to select plants for a courtyard garden from a huge range to suit both these extremes and the varying degrees of sun and shade found in between.

Courtyard walls also provide an un-rivalled opportunity to plant in a vertical dimension, lending height, structure, and colour with climbers and wall shrubs.

COOL COURTYARD
With a trelliswork screen for wind shelter and privacy, potted plants are placed to take best advantage of higher light levels, while large-leaved shade-tolerant plants, like Fatsia japonica, *grow lush and verdant, thriving in the still, humid air against a partly shaded wall.*

WIND TUNNELS

Courtyards and, to a lesser extent, patios, may experience a wind-tunnel effect. A wind tunnel occurs when wind strikes two adjacent solid objects and is forced through the gap between them. The result is an increase in wind velocity, which can be detrimental to plant growth and unpleasant for people. Similarly, wind hitting a lower, solid object, such as a close-boarded fence, is forced over the top, again increasing wind speed, but also creating eddies, or turbulence, behind the object.

In both cases, the best solution is to interpose a perforated, rather than a solid, barrier between you and the wind. This will allow some air to filter through, thus avoiding turbulence, but will greatly reduce the overall wind speed.

Simple trellis panels are effective if the problem is relatively minor, but you may need to consider a palisade fence with gaps between the boards, an informal deciduous or evergreen hedge, or a screen of large shrubs where the problem is greater.

FILTERS AND BARRIERS

• A wind-filtering screen will create shelter in its lee for a distance equal to about five times its height.

• In a new garden, you could consider using a temporary screen of a proprietary plastic mesh, or woven, willow hurdles until the plantings have reached sufficient stature to do the job alone.

Provided that they do not cut out too much sun, or create excessive rainshadows, tall barriers will reduce the effects of wind over much greater distances than short ones.

When planning your patio or courtyard, it is important to take account of any potential wind tunnels. And it is equally important, if considering building new walls, to try to site them so as not to create new wind tunnels.

SCREENING AGAINST THE WIND
A sturdy, latticework panel filters the wind without creating turbulence; as it becomes clothed with climbing plants, its effect is enhanced still further.

▶ DAPPLED SHADE
The dappled shade cast by trees can be a pleasure to sit beneath on a hot day. Here, potentially dense shade has been alleviated by clearing low branches from the tree in the corner of the garden (top right) to form a high canopy that admits light below it.

▼ SHADE LOVER
The tough and tolerant Lesser periwinkle, Vinca minor, *is a perfect planting solution for dry, shady areas and makes excellent ground cover.*

SUN, SHADE, AND RAINSHADOWS

Relieving excessive shade will depend primarily on its cause. If it is created by a solid, vertical wall, you might lighten it up by painting it white, or perhaps introducing bright splashes of colour with variegated plants or painted ornaments.

Beneath a large shrub or tree, shade can be reduced to a degree by removing some of the lower branches on the trunk. The best solution may be to remove a tree entirely, which may reveal a previously hidden view. But you must always check first that the tree is not subject to a local authority preservation order.

Rainshadows are dry zones found on the downwind side of walls, solid fences, or hedges, where rain penetrates only in windless conditions (*see also p.53*). They are seen most clearly after rain following a dry period. Plant shrubs and climbers some

way out from the wall or fence, improve the soil with organic matter, and be prepared to irrigate in very dry periods.

Replacing a solid fence with a more open one will allow at least some rain to percolate through. Hedges, especially coniferous ones, exacerbate the problem

Rainshadows provide a perfect spot for drought-tolerant plants

with their greedy root systems. They can be root-pruned annually, or you could save labour by paving a rain shadow area rather than planting it. Alternatively, you could fill it with drought-tolerant plants. Sun-loving bulbs, like nerines, welcome dry conditions, especially when they are dormant.

A STYLE TO SUIT YOUR TASTE

WHAT IS THE DIFFERENCE between taste and style? Style refers to something that might be universally recognized – Impressionism or Art Deco, for example. Taste is more personal and may, or may not, coincide with any one style and, indeed, may be a combination of several. Ultimately, your design must satisfy your needs above all else, so exploit other garden ideas for inspiration, by all means, but adapt them to create something that is uniquely your own.

SEEKING INSPIRATION

Fireside perusal of books, magazines, and other media is ideal for the darker winter months, but undoubtedly, the best source of inspiration is to view gardens in the flesh.

They may be private gardens, open for only one or two days a year for charity, grand historic gardens, or botanic gardens and horticultural education establishments with a wide range of plants and, perhaps, display gardens. At the cutting edge are the large flower and garden shows and exhibitions, which nearly always show both ultra-modern and traditional styles.

In the best gardens, you will get a real feel for the scale and qualities of the living plants and you can view a wide range of other features, which act as an excellent and inspirational guide when you put your own design on the ground.

WHAT ARE THE OPTIONS?

Whether your taste is best expressed by adopting a formal style, with angular symmetry and crisp planting, or your preference is for a looser, informal style with curves and softer lines, is entirely your choice. You may decide to combine aspects of both to satisfy your desires, but one of the keys to great design is to embrace simplicity and avoid over-complication.

The hard landscaping – paving, walls, and paths, forms the framework of nearly all designs. Choosing one single material,

ULTRA MODERN
The clean, sharp lines of this ultra-modern courtyard garden form a unified whole with the home that encloses it. Blond wood, pale stone, and polished metal accord perfectly with the formal setting, so that nothing jars or appears out of place.

TRADITIONAL
Roses round the door may fulfil your dream if you are a real traditionalist at heart. The abundance and soft lines of the plantings are artlessly informal and, in keeping with the style, plants are allowed to spill gently over onto a crisp sweep of gravel.

such as brick or stone, or one colour range for structural elements provides a unifying theme that helps prevent the design from appearing fragmented or fussy. And a strong background allows you much more scope for variety in your plantings.

Colour-themed plantings can determine the mood of the garden. Cool blues, greys, and greens are refreshing and lend depth and perspective. Pastel pinks, yellows, and lilacs are warm and relaxing, while hot oranges, reds, and golds demand attention.

Movement adds another dimension. Tall grasses shimmer in the wind, revealing the often coloured undersides to their leaves as they do so. Water features lend sound and movement, with a glimmer of reflected light and restful murmurs. You can use wind-driven sculptures of glass or polished metal to achieve the same effect.

▲ USING SCULPTURE
Beyond and above mere decoration, these bronze pigs also express the gentle sense of humour of their owner.

◄ RUNNING WATER
Using a traditional fountain spout in an ultra-modern setting proves a winning combination of styles.

FRAME AND FILL

In both courtyards and patios, it is almost inevitable that a considerable amount of floor space is taken up by paving materials.

With only a limited area left for planting, the ideal policy is to choose plants that both give plenty of value and do not outgrow their allotted space. As an essential part of the framework, use evergreen shrubs, for example, to guarantee year-round foliage interest and seasonal flowers. Try deciduous, flowering shrubs with variegated or coloured foliage, like *Weigela florida* 'Aureovariegata', to extend the colour range. If placed with care to avoid problems of excessive growth and shade, many small trees, like Crab apples (*Malus* sp.), are perfect for lending height, as well as flowers and fruit at various times of year. And many plants with coloured bark or stems, like *Cornus alba* 'Sibirica', can be used to brighten the winter months.

A structural framework of woody plants forms a backdrop for a softer, seasonally changing infill of perennials, bulbs and annuals. Perennials with a prolonged season of bloom, like *Anemone* × *hybrida* 'Honorine Jobert', or flowerheads that age gracefully, such as *Sedum spectabile*, give great value. But you can also prolong interest with successional underplantings.

POINT AND COUNTERPOINT

- Include bold-leaved plants, like *Acanthus mollis*, or *Verbascum olympicum*, to make dramatic focal points.

- Use variations in habit to add interest and contrast – perhaps a tall column of a grass like *Miscanthus*, alongside a low, evergreen dome of *Skimmia japonica* 'Rubella'.

- Set contrasting foliage textures side-by-side, for example, feathery astilbes against large-leaved hostas, or spiky-leaved yuccas against plump-leaved sedums.

▲ PLANTING WITH PURPOSE
While suffusing the air with perfume, climbing roses and honeysuckles provide welcome shade from the hottest summer sun.

▶ COLOUR CONTRAST
A great all-rounder, the dark-leaved cherry, (Prunus cerasifera 'Nigra'), lends sheltering height and summer-long foliage contrast, with the added benefit of pink blossom in spring.

Try a summer-flowering *Hibiscus syriacus*, for example, underplanted with *Dicentra spectabilis* 'Alba', which flowers over a long period in late spring, with bulbs like *Chionodoxa* beneath, adding starry blue flowers in early spring.

SAVING GRACE
Any plants that prevent weed growth by covering the ground represent a good investment if you have only limited time for garden maintenance. Traditional, low ground cover, such as ivy (*Hedera*) and lesser periwinkle (*Vinca minor*), can be very efficient and is excellent in both sun and partial shade beneath shrubs. But ground-cover plants do not have to be prostrate or evergreen. Daylilies (*Hemerocallis*) and shrubby potentillas (*Potentilla fruticosa*) have dense, weed-excluding growth as well as height, attractive form, and flowering periods that last through much of summer.

SMALL TREES

Arbutus unedo Evergreen, with attractive bark, bell-shaped white flowers and small red fruits, both borne in autumn.

Betula albosinensis Peeling, orange-brown bark, and rich yellow autumn foliage.

Crataegus pedicellata White flowers in late spring; good autumn colour with long-lasting, bright red fruit (haws).

Sorbus cashmeriana White flowers in spring; good autumn colour and hanging clusters of white berries in autumn.

Sorbus vilmorinii White flowers in late spring; the dark red berries in autumn turn pink and age to white; good autumn colour.

***Prunus* × *subhirtella* 'Autumnalis'** Good autumn colour and white or pink flowers, borne intermittently in mild periods between autumn and spring.

CONFINED TO BOUNDS
Training climbing and scrambling plants on sturdy trelliswork confines them to the vertical so they do not encroach on valuable space.

PLANS FOR PATIOS AND COURTYARDS

A SELECTION OF WORKING DESIGNS

THE DESIGN YOU FINALLY CREATE for your own patio or courtyard will, of course, reflect your own personal style and lifestyle. The plans on the following pages aim to inspire and reveal the art of the possible. They address many of the design problems that are common to such restricted spaces, including tips on how to make them seem larger. You will find a positive wealth of ideas here to select from, combine, and adapt to suit your own site.

WHAT IS YOUR PROBLEM?

The plans show how to deal with a hot spot (p.24), make the most of a cool, shady one (p.26), or deal with difficult sites, like a long, narrow garden (p.32), or a steeply sloping one (p.42). You may have a concrete desert that needs a makeover (p.38), perhaps by transforming it to lush jungle (p.46) – the solutions are here.

If modern life leaves you yearning to restore the balance, a private space (pp.34, 40), or a little aromatherapy (p.30) might be just the ticket. How better to unwind than dining *al fresco* with friends (p.36). And if you want to combine your more sophisticated needs with those of the children, see p.28. You might even grow your own provisions together (p.44).

TINY COURTYARD
The tiniest space can be transformed into a fine place for peaceful relaxation. It can also be one that needs the minimum of work to maintain once you have made the initial effort. Even a total lack of open soil will not prevent you from growing a few carefully chosen plants in pots.

◄ ALL YOU NEED *A sunny patio, a little shade, and no lawn to mow.*

A Hot, Dry Patio

Hot, dry areas can be very attractive to sit in, but there are times when heat becomes overwhelming and some cool shade is desirable. This patio makes the best of both worlds, with a central paved area in full sun – surrounded by plants that thrive in dry heat. It is linked to more paving beneath a timber pergola that is clothed in climbers and backed by tall shrubs to create a contrasting, cool, shady site. A drilled boulder water feature set amongst cobbles and pebbles provides a focal point, adds atmospheric humidity, and provides the pleasing sight and sounds of moving water. It is thoughtfully designed to have no standing water, so that it is safe for small children.

Hot corner for taller sun-loving plants like ceanothus, sage, and artemisias

Pale-coloured paving forms a firm surface and a strong, unifying element throughout the design

Pergola with timber crossbeams provides overhead shade from the hottest midday sun

Exposed aggregate flags are attractive and non-slip, especially if colonized by algae in shady spots

Tall urn for sun-loving bulbs such as scented lilies, or long-flowering perennials like agapanthus

A table for four with adequate space for free movement all around includes a shade umbrella for comfortable dining

Drilled boulder is fitted with fountain spout. Surrounded by cobbles and lined with pebbles, there is no depth of standing water

Foliage of shrubby *Berberis thunbergii* 'Rose Glow', in warm reds, is offset by the blue-leaved grass, *Festuca glauca*, in the foreground

Sweep of gravel abuts paving and, laid on geotextile membrane, makes a low-maintenance, "no-mow" surface

Containers of varying heights and widths provide visual variety and a home for heat-loving plants like sempervivums

N

DESIGN BRIEF

• To exploit the positive aspects of dry heat while alleviating the more uncomfortable aspects of a hot spot by providing some shade.
• To provide a firm, paved surface for seating and occasional dining.
• To provide a safe, moving water feature for cool humidity.
• To include readily available, easily grown drought- and heat-tolerant plants, in open ground and containers.

Trellis provides privacy, shelter, and support for climbers, like *Actinidia kolomikta* and fragrant, climbing roses

Shaded area planted with shade-bearing shrubs, such as *Mahonia* × *media* and fuchsias, underplanted with ground-covering *Lamium maculatum*

A bench seat located beneath the pergola can be moved, as necessary, to make the most of shade throughout the day

Tall shrubs, including *Buddleja davidii*, *Elaeagnus pungens* 'Maculata', *Hibiscus syriacus*, and *Berberis* × *ottawensis* 'Superba', lend shade and shelter

Tall grasses, like *Miscanthus sacchariflorus* and *Stipa gigantea*, provide screening as well as sound and movement in the slightest breeze

Edging of *Sedum spectabile* provides foliage interest for spring and summer, and flowers attract basking butterflies in late summer

PERGOLAS FOR SHADE

Pergolas are a great way of providing cool shade and privacy. A pergola is a series of vertical posts or piers made from wood, stone or brick, supporting a system of horizontal rails or arches, usually of wood or metal, above head height. Verticals must be set firmly in the ground (usually a minimum depth of 45cm/18in), and if stone or brick is used, the pillars must have a suitable foundation.

◀ IN SCALE
Headroom beneath a pergola should be about 2.1m (7ft); any less feels oppressive. Make the width between posts not less than 1.2m (4ft) over a path, or 1.8m (6ft) in a sitting-out area.

▼ IN PROPORTION
Here, slender uprights give support without being unduly intrusive on the ground. For tiny pergolas, small-gauge metal, wrought iron, or lightweight wood sections are ideal. Use brick or stone piers with oak beams for larger ones.

A SHADY COURTYARD

MANY COURTYARDS ARE SURROUNDED by high walls and buildings and, in some cases, direct sunlight never touches the ground, although it may brighten the upper reaches of one or more walls. In this design, plants that thrive in damp shade form a framework around an open area of brick-edged, exposed aggregate concrete and gravel. Exposed aggregate and riven stone flags are chosen for their rough, non-slip surfaces and flags are spaced to provide planting niches between them. Pale paving and white-painted walls are used for their ability to reflect light and the pale walls are mirrored in the calm surface of the formal pool.

Golden-leaved *Philadelphus coronarius* 'Aureus' keeps foliage colour best in shade

Stepping stones reinforce the optical illusion created by white-painted *faux* gateway that brightens dull wall

Formal pond is located centrally in an area that receives good overhead light, to maximize reflections

Boulders and random cobbles of a slightly darker hue break up an expanse of gravel and make fine contrasts with it

For plantings in shade, ferns like dryopteris and perennials such as dicentras, astilbes, brunneras, and filipendulas predominate

Dark corner is brightened by gold-speckled leaves of *Aucuba japonica* 'Crotonifolia'

Architectural outline of the fern, *Matteuccia struthiopteris*, is reflected in still water

Pale-flowered climber, *Schizophragma hydrangeoides*, brightens dark wall

Apple-green leaves of bamboo, *Fargesia murieliae*, form backdrop for terracotta urns

DESIGN BRIEF

• A design to alleviate the potential gloom of a shaded courtyard, by using pale coloured hard landscaping materials.
• To use paving materials that provide a surface that is safe and non-slip when damp.
• To include a diversity of shade-bearing plants with a long or multiple season of interest.
• To provide an element of vertical interest with climbers on walls and wall supports.

Pale-flowered shrubs, *Hydrangea villosa,* and *H. macrophylla* 'Lanarth White' underplanted with silver-leaved *Pulmonaria saccharata* Argentea Group

The best-lit area of the courtyard is raised and used for a seating area and made brighter by white-painted furniture and pale paving

Brick edging makes a fine decorative detail and a retaining edge for poured (*in situ*) exposed aggregate concrete

Random-sized, rectangular flags set in gravel with gravel infill in crevices allows for future planting between them

Matching the patio border, a circular area of light-coloured gravel and brick pavers forms a standing area for three Cretan terracotta urns, forming a fine focal point

ALLEVIATING THE GLOOM

There are some excellent flowering and foliage plants, such as hydrangeas and *Euonymus fortunei* cultivars, that will brighten dark corners, but there are many more that do not make much of an impact when seen against a dark, sunless wall. Painting vertical surfaces in white or pale colours makes a better backdrop for plants and reflects light back to lift the gloom. Additional light spots can be created with painted, pale-coloured trellis, mirrors, or *trompe l'oeil* doorways, arches, or windows.

▲ BRIGHT COLOURS *Pale paving and trellis help lift this shady courtyard out of the gloom, but it is the bright blues of the furniture, echoed in a tiled wall mosaic, that really make it sparkle.*

◀ WHITE WALLS *Crisp, clean and sparkling white, the walls will maximize reflected light. Just a day's work applying whitewash each year in spring will keep it looking pristine.*

AN ENCLOSED FAMILY COURTYARD

DESIGNING A SMALL GARDEN TO MEET the sometimes conflicting needs of family members can be a challenge. This design provides open space for children to run around and play in, as well as attractive features to suit sophisticated adult tastes. A bold, geometric ground plan includes bricks for edging and low retaining walls create raised planting beds behind. The patio area is in sun – by the kitchen door for easy supervision – and durable, boxed-in seats double as storage for toys and garden tools. A neat sand pit has a removable cover to keep out cats and there is a generous play area mulched with play bark to ensure soft landings.

Safe shrubs include purple-leaved *Weigela florida* 'Foliis Purpureis' and variegated sage, *Salvia officinalis* 'Tricolor'

Sand pit filled with washed sand or silver sand to avoid staining clothes; it must be lime-free to avoid skin burns

Raised beds give some protection to plants that might otherwise be damaged by rough play

Wall fitted with trellis to accommodate fragrant climbing roses

Butterflies attracted by *Buddleja* 'Lochinch', will fascinate adults and children alike

Shady pergola with seating beneath is clothed in fragrant wisteria for pure relaxation or close supervision of childrens' play

Play bark makes a safe surface for graze-free landings; do not use ordinary chipped bark which can splinter and cause injury

DESIGN BRIEF

• An enclosed back yard to accommodate a safe childrens' play area and outdoor dining and entertaining for adults.

• Child-safe water feature, play surfaces and a sand pit that is covered when not in use (to exclude cats; fouling carries a risk of *Toxicara* infection that can cause blindness).

• Durable plantings of non-toxic, non-spiny, non-irritant plants that do not bear tempting berries or seed pods.

Boxed-in bench seating with lift-up lid to store garden tools and play equipment

Durable table and seating for *al fresco* dining and entertaining suits both adults and children alike

Late summer flowers of *Hydrangea* 'Preziosa' can be pressed or dried and used for collages or other artwork for rainy-day play

Fine-textured, non-slip surface of small brick pavers is suitable for play with wheeled toys and small pedal tricycles

Drilled boulder water feature has a cobble surround and recirculating water powered by low-voltage pump; it is easily visible from house

Brick edging laid flush with play bark surface, thus avoiding a step that could lead to trips and falls

SAFETY FIRST

Non-toxic plants and safe, non-slip surfaces are *de rigeur* in childrens' gardens. Where children have free access, water features must be designed with safety in mind. A traditional pond can be made safer by setting a cover of builder's steel reinforcing mesh an inch or so below the surface, but even this carries a risk. Safer still is to create a feature that has no depth of standing water at all.

▲ WOODEN DECKING
If decking is on the wish list in an area that children will use, it should be made of grooved (reeded) hardwood which is less slippery than smooth wood and less likely to splinter.

▼ CHILD-FRIENDLY WATER
A recirculating feature recycles water from a sump via a pump and hidden pipes. The sump is safely covered with fine mesh topped by cobbles; this also helps keep water free of debris.

THE FRAGRANT COURTYARD

ONE OF THE MOST APPEALING QUALITIES of a courtyard is the relatively still air found there, which allows the scent of plants to linger and not be dispersed quickly by the breeze. This design places strong emphasis on fragrance at various times of year and includes several pretty features in a small space without being cramped or fussy. There is a generous area of paving with room for furniture to allow outdoor dining and entertaining. Height is provided by climbers on a pergola, on arches, and an arbour, while at lower levels, a chamomile lawn and plantings in raised beds ensure perfume rises from the ground.

Small tree, *Malus* 'Golden Hornet' with scented white flowers in spring and yellow crab apples to follow

Fragrance in late winter and early spring provided by *Clematis cirrhosa* var. *balearica* on wall trellis

Raised bed brings perfumes of *Mahonia × media* 'Winter Sun', *Syringa meyeri* 'Palibin', nicotianas and stocks closer to "nose-level"

Fan-shaped pergola provides shade and supports *Wisteria floribunda* for scented, early summer flowers

Wrought iron arch supports *Rosa* 'Aloha' with scented flowers over a very long season

Gravel planted with scented thymes and lavenders

Arbour clothed in scented roses and sweet peas (*Lathyrus odoratus*)

DESIGN BRIEF

• A design that exploits the still air of a sheltered courtyard to capture plant fragrances.
• To include a range of features to lend height variation and provide scent at every level from the ground upwards.
• To provide plenty of space for comfortable outdoor dining and entertaining.
• To include a water feature to enhance humidity, and to lend the sight and sound of moving water.

Table and chairs for six people in pale-coloured hardwood

Generous area of random rectangular stone flags allows ample space for outdoor dining

Chamomile lawn (*Chamaemelum nobilis* 'Treneague') constrained by barley twist edging tiles

Small raised pool with fountain spout enhances humidity and helps air retain fragrance

Arch supports highly scented climber, *Jasminum officinale* var. *affine*, blooming from summer to autumn

THE SCENTED CARPET

The idea of a fragrant carpet of plants is by no means new. The traditional choice is a non-flowering chamomile, *Chamaemelum nobile* 'Treneague'; its fruity scent is released when the foliage is trodden lightly. Plant at 15cm (6in) spacings in well-drained soil in sun and trim with shears in spring and again in midsummer. Many low-growing thymes succeed equally well with similar treatment.

CREEPING THYMES
Low, spreading thymes, like this Thymus serpyllum *variety, will withstand some treading and are ideal for planting in paving crevices or in gravel.*

CLOVE-SCENTED PINKS
Many pinks, like this 'Haytor White' have a distinctive clove scent. Exploit their low, dense habit to provide fragrant edging to the border.

FRAGRANT PAVING
Leaving paving crevices without mortar gives the ideal opportunity for interplanting with scented plants, like thyme and marjoram, which release their scents when gently brushed against in passing.

A PATIO IN A LONG, NARROW GARDEN

THE CLAUSTROPHOBIC, CORRIDOR-LIKE EFFECT of a long, narrow garden is a common design problem. Here, the problem is eliminated by the clever device of turning the patio through 45° and arranging a path to run back and forth down the garden in a series of doglegs. Flagstones divided by brick strips emphasize the angular aspect of the patio and a screen, divided into window-like compartments, breaks up the long view down the garden and defines a series of intimate spaces. Ugly outbuilding walls are softened and hidden by climbers and wall shrubs. A raised formal pool makes a striking feature – offset to one side of the patio – while its wide coping provides additional, occasional seating.

To screen unattractive boundary wall, an evergreen shrub, *Ceanothus* 'Delight', with deep blue flowers in mid- to late spring, is trained against the wall

Trellis fixed to walls of outbuilding support a disguising screen of an evergreen climber, *Clematis cirrhosa* var. *balearica*

A formal pool, offset to emphasise diagonals, has a wide stone coping to provide additional seating and the opportunity to observe plants and pond life at close quarters

An interrupted screen of trellis panels allows glimpses through to the garden beyond and defines the patio space

Pale-coloured flagstones reflect as much as heat and warmth as possible back into the patio area

French windows give access to the patio and views from the house into the garden

Brindle bricks, laid on the diagonal, break up the regular paving flags and emphasize the angular aspect of the patio

DESIGN BRIEF

• A design to break up the long, narrow space into a series of garden "rooms' that will provide a sense of intimate enclosure and invite exploration beyond.

• To include a patio for dining and entertaining with easy access to and from the house.

• To incorporate a formal pool that will also allow additional, occasional seating

• To include plantings of tall shrubs and climbers to screen off the unsightly outbuilding walls.

Two arches, clothed with roses and clematis, are set at right angles to form an enclosure by linking two runs of trellis screening

Ornamental statue rises above a sea of flowers and foliage, creating a focal point at the end of a vista from the seating area on the patio

Interrupted trellis screening encloses patio and provides privacy for bench seating

Secluded bench seating in a second garden room, faces down the garden to enjoy the long view down the garden

Gravel surface allows interplanting with fragrant plants

BREAKING UP THE SPACE

One of the devices used by garden designers to deal with the problems found in long, narrow gardens is to break up the view down the garden with some form of screen. Fenestrated screening – a screen with "windows" in it – is a good choice for this purpose. It allows glimpses through it, inviting further exploration of the garden, but avoids the sense of claustrophobic enclosure of a more solid screen.

▲ USING FENESTRATED SCREENING
Here, peep-through screens of light, airy trellis effectively divide a long corridor into more intimate spaces of pleasing proportions.

▶ MIRROR MAGIC
This variation on the theme of windowed screens uses a mirror to lend the illusion of hidden space beyond the arch that frames it. It also reflects light and removes the sense of confinement that a blank wall would bring to the restricted space.

A Patio in Informal Style

THE SQUARE OR RECTANGULAR PATIO so often found with new houses is discarded in this design in favour of a more dynamic, organic layout. The sweeping curves of a brick patio swing round to lead onto a path to the far end of the garden. At the rear of the patio is a stone bird bath backed by a curved, wrought iron screen. Water cascades down three stainless steel dishes to form the centre point of an almost circular seating area. Curved arches, raised beds, and a broad sweep of lawn reinforce the theme and informal plantings curl around an intimate seating area, surrounding it with scent, colour, and textural contrasts.

Raised beds in blue-brindled brick echo and accentuate the curves of the patio

Small brick pavers that form patio are laid in a pattern of long, sinuous curves

Blue and white canvas loungers chosen to match the blue brick of the raised beds

A series of three broad, curved arches clothed in scented climbers surround a bench seat

Recirculating cascade of water spills over the rims of circular, stainless steel dishes on three levels

Smooth, water-worn cobbles set in mortar edge the fountain feature and a path of stone chippings or gravel

To provide intimate, partial enclosure, border has plantings of graduated height; a tall rhododendron at the back, down to creeping bugle (*Ajuga reptans*) at the front

Lawn area turfed with fine grass can be mown in curved stripes

N

DESIGN BRIEF

- A design based on dynamic curves to break away from the more traditional four-square patio abutting the house.
- To accentuate a theme of curves in aerial features, like screens and arches, and in focal elements, such as a fountain and bird bath.
- To provide secluded seating surrounded by luxuriant plantings.
- To use materials that can be laid easily in curved forms.

Stone bird bath on raised stone plinth sits above the level of planting to avoid leafy debris collecting in it

Blue-painted, wrought iron screen clothed in clematis curves around bird bath and forms an elegant backdrop to it

Trellis screen provides support for climbing roses and clematis and disguises boundary wall

Mixed border with more than one season of interest, includes: *Juniperus chinensis* 'Aurea', *Viburnum opulus* 'Compactum', Japanese anemones, *Iris pallida* 'Argentea Variegata'

Patio area merges with a brick path that leads to the rest of the garden

FORMING CURVES WITH PAVERS

While large, square, or rectangular pavers are perfect for straight-edged layouts, they are less suitable for creating smooth curves. Even with extensive cutting, the overall effect is still predominantly angular. With smaller units, such as half-sized bricks, clay pavers, setts, or cobbles, you can produce tighter, more variable curves, giving much more freedom in creating the shapes you desire.

◀ FORMING CIRCLES
A circular frame for a fountain is formed by mortared half-bricks and loose cobbles. Note the extensive cutting needed to shape the square tiles.

▼ LAYING CURVES
For the best effects when laying small clay pavers in curves, the joints between them, whether filled with mortar, sand, or grit, should be kept as small and uniform as possible.

A Patio for Outdoor Dining

THE PRE-REQUISITES FOR SUCCESSFUL OUTDOOR DINING are that there should be adequate space for the purpose, shelter – as far as possible – from the worst of the elements, and a location that is conveniently near to a preparation area for food and drink. This scheme fits that bill with a generous expanse of decking that adjoins both kitchen and dining room. A roller blind awning can be pulled over part of the deck, if needed, and a combination of trellis screens covered in climbers and tall shrubs encloses the area and provides shelter from prevailing winds. The barbecue is just far enough away to avoid smoke nuisance at the dining table and low- and high-level lighting enhance the ambience at night.

House wall forms firm fixing point for retractable, self-supporting awning (*not shown*). A self-supporting model has no vertical posts that might get in the way

Low-level lighting, with translucent shades, provides glare-free safety lighting either side of step into house

Box seats sit three or four and, with hinged, lift-up lids, they double as outdoor storage areas for barbecue equipment

Low-level lighting is placed to illuminate a change of level between deck and garden

Warm-coloured timber decking boards, which are grooved (reeded) for a non-slip surface

Geyser fountain is illuminated at night with the subtle glow of submerged lighting

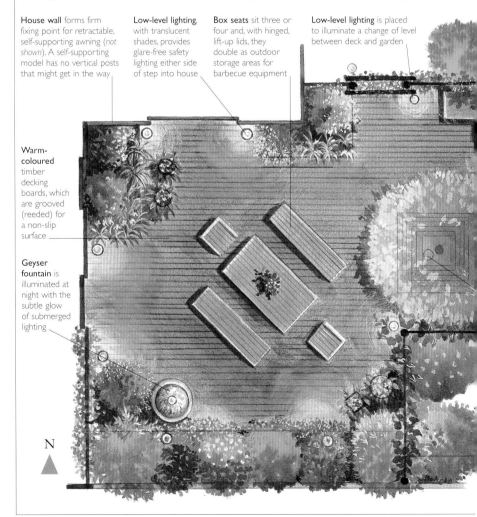

N

Barbecue and preparation area sited away from dining table in a corner that is sheltered from prevailing winds

Small tree is illuminated from below using a spot-beamed uplighter that is focussed away from diners to avoid glare

Trellis screen clothed with climbers and with tall shrubs to the fore provides shelter from the prevailing winds

UNDER CANVAS

Umbrellas or parasols are excellent for creating instant shade over outdoor furniture and can be moved around to give great flexibility. They are, however, less useful in protecting against rain. If you spend a lot of time on the patio, you might consider an awning that covers a larger area and provides some shelter from showers. A fixed, retractable awning is one option, but if this is too permanent, consider using a free-standing garden canopy with curtain sides; they are very light, easy to erect, and most are suitable for use on areas of hard standing or grass.

▲ AWNING
A retractable awning can be extended on rainy, or very hot days, to provide shelter or shade. The metal framework has a small "footprint" that does not intrude on the dining space.

◀ SHADE UMBRELLA
Although an elegant and flexible means of warding off the sun, unless ther is no wind, umbrellas offer only limited protection from showers.

BARE YARD TO COURTYARD

NOT ALL BACKYARDS ARE BLESSED WITH ample topsoil and some consist of little more than an area of concrete, tarmac, or a hard-packed mixture of rubble. If you are unable – or unwilling – to incur the major expense and upheaval of removing this material, you can still create a stunning garden by building on what you have. This design uses raised beds for the main plantings and a selection of pots for both permanent and seasonal displays. A pergola provides a lightly shaded area and a means of support for hanging baskets. To provide sound and movement, a water spout cascades into a wall-mounted, half-moon pool.

Trelliswork is fixed to wall above the raised bed to support climbers, such as *Clematis* 'Henryi', with creamy-white flowers in summer

A depth of at least a metre (yard) of good soil permits planting of shrubs and even a small tree, here, the red-leaved Japanese maple, *Acer palmatum* 'Bloodgood'

Here, sufficient material could be excavated to allow levelling of area for laying paving, but had this been impossible, decking or gravel could be laid directly onto the existing ground

Raised bed in natural oak has built-in, bench seating in same material. Note the gap of 75mm (3in) between wall and raised bed to allow free ventilation behind

Selection of containers for seasonally changing or permanent plantings

Wall-mounted fountain spout cascades into a raised, brick-built, butyl-lined, half-moon pool

Random rectangular stone-effect paving is bordered by contrasting, blue-brindled brick pavers

DESIGN BRIEF

• A makeover of a
soilless yard that has no
open ground at all.
• To include a moving
water feature.
• To include ample
seating.
• A pergola to lend
height and shade.
• To create a range of
planting opportunities;
raised beds for shrub
and tree plantings and
containers of varying
size for seasonally
changing ones, with
larger ones to
accommodate climbers.

Natural oak pergola
has uprights set
into paving and
crosspieces are fixed
to the boundary
wall with fixing
plates or joist shoes

Planting holes are
excavated and filled
with compost or
good topsoil to
accommodate the
climbers that clothe
trellis. Hanging baskets
are suspended from
crosspieces of pergola

N

Stone troughs or
wooden planters
provide planting sites
for shade-bearing
wall climbers

Raised beds are
constructed of natural
oak timbers with a
perforated plastic liner
and weep holes at the
base to allow drainage

USING RAISED BEDS

Raised beds are a good way of overcoming the problem of
inadequate topsoil. By choosing the finished height with care and
ensuring that the width is not excessive, they are easy to tend, even
for gardeners of limited mobility. Make sure that raised beds have
good drainage, either via seepholes at the base, or directly into the
ground below and that they are filled with good quality topsoil,
improved, if possible, with organic matter.

▲ WOODEN BEDS
*Use only preservative-treated
timbers for raised beds and line
them with perforated plastic to
permit good drainage and
protect the wood from rotting
after contact with damp soil.*

▼ CONCRETE STRUCTURE
*Concrete is a versatile building
medium; raised beds can be
constructed from pre-cast
concrete kerbing, or poured in
situ into wooden formers to
create the shape you desire.*

A PATIO FOR PRIVACY

HAVING A PATIO NEXT TO THE HOUSE is, as a rule, a good idea in terms of
practicalities and convenience. There are times, however, when a patio in a
secluded location, perhaps at the bottom of the garden, is desirable on account of
the privacy it affords. In this design, the potential inconvenience of a distant patio
is overcome by having a summerhouse with its own electricity supply, a barbecue
and built-in storage cupboard, and a set of durable, all-weather patio furniture.
The patio is hidden from neighbours by perimeter plantings of shrubs and
climbers and staggered wooden screens
hide the area from the rest of the
garden, but still permit easy access.

Trellis screen planted with
Hedera helix 'Goldheart'
trained across the mesh;
outward growing shoots
are clipped back from time
to time to keep the screen
dense and tight

Second trellis screen is
staggered and offset
to hide the patio from
view from the rest of
the garden and a
raised bed forms a
planting site for the
climber that clothes it

Summerhouse with
wooden shingle roof;
it has its own water
supply and a mains
electricity supply fitted by
a professional electrician

Durable, all-weather
patio furniture can
be left outdoors all
year round, or stored
in the summerhouse
in winter, if necessary

Barbecue has built-in
work surface for food
preparation and a store
cupboard beneath for
cooking utensils and
other equipment

DESIGN BRIEF

- A patio to provide privacy; the garden adjacent to the house is overlooked by neighbours, is draughty, and does not receive much sun.
- Needs clean, all-weather access between the patio and house.
- Must include durable furniture that does not have to be dragged to and from the house when not in use.
- A combined, paved barbecue, dining, and seating area.

Tall, rustling grasses, provide a supplemental screen in front of trellis covered with clipped ivy (*Hedera helix* 'Green Ripple')

Small tree, *Acer negundo* 'Flamingo', screens patio from overlooking neighbours

Plain, pale-coloured rectangular flags provide clean, all-weather access that is continued, as a path, back to the house

Ornamental statue forms a focal point and is backed by trellis screen supporting a climbing rose and flanked by fragrant mock orange (*Philadelphus*)

N

CLEVER WAYS WITH SCREENS

Screens are used to create privacy, to block unwanted views, as wind or sun breaks, or as a means of dividing the garden up into rooms. If trellis is set at an angle of 45° to the line of vision, the gaps between the lathes appear smaller, making a more effective screen. To block a view, plant a screen of shrubs across the line of sight and divert any paths around one or both sides of the barrier.

◄ LIVING SCREENS
The canopies of trees are ideal for screening a garden that is overlooked; they take up relatively little ground space and if they cast undue shade, this can be alleviated by pruning off the lower branches.

▼ SOLID SCREENS
Although costly to build, a high, peep-proof, stone or brick wall provides the ultimate means of securing privacy and a sense of intimate enclosure in a garden.

A PATIO FOR A SLOPING GARDEN

To MAKE A SLOPING GARDEN USABLE, you will need to terrace it in order to form one or more level areas suitable for your intended purposes – to provide a site for a patio, lawn, or plantings, for example. The terraces of this garden, which slopes away from the house, are retained by low brick walls that are built as part-circles; as with a building arch, curved walls are stronger than straight ones. The curved theme is continued by the brick-edged planting beds, the semi-circular pool that is fed from the terrace above, and the meandering bark path that leads to the top of the garden. Small trees and large shrubs are carefully placed to break up the view and to create different vistas as you move around the garden.

Crushed bark path, laid on top of a geotextile membrane, meanders across the terraces to the top of the garden

A spreading, small tree, *Malus floribunda*, is sited to break up the view from the patio; it has pink flowers in spring, followed by tiny yellow crab apples

In this tiny garden, there is no obvious place for storage, so durable, all-weather furniture, like this teak table and chairs, is absolutely essential

Wooden planters with climbing roses and clematis trained up a screen of trellis that disguises the boundary wall

N

Steps incorporated into wall for access between levels

Small tree, *Koelreuteria paniculata*, screens the patio from neighbours

A focal point, *Phormium tenax* 'Dazzler', emphasizes the change in level

DESIGN BRIEF

- A design to convert a slope that rises steeply away from the house into a usable space for planting and for a level patio adjacent to the house.
- To include a water cascade.
- To include plantings that screen the patio from without and create new vistas within the garden.
- To provide access to the garden from the patio by means of paths and steps.

Random, rectangular stone flags form the patio surface, the sub-base has been excavated so that the finished surface is 15cm (6in) below the damp proof course

Semi-circular pool is brick-built and lined with butyl liner. Fountain spout cascades into it from the level above and is re-circulated via pump and hidden pipework

Terraces interfere with natural drainage down the slope and put added stress on the wall. Drainage is ensured by a gentle fall across terrace with a weep hole to the level below; at the lowest level, a French drain is linked to a soakaway

Ground-level planting beds with curved edge in brick; avoid raised beds next to house walls as they breach the damp course

RETAINING WALLS

When you terrace a sloping garden you are, in effect, cutting out giant steps (*see p. 51*). To support the vertical face of the steps, a retaining wall is needed, otherwise the steps will revert quickly to a slope under the force of gravity. On gentle slopes, where the change of level is only about 15–30cm (6–12in), a single brick wall, or a series of treated logs driven vertically into the soil, may be adequate. If the level change is substantially more, the strength and stability of the wall is critical and, unless you are skilled and experienced in building work, you should seek professional advice.

▲ ON THE TERRACE
Here, terracing has created a level area next to the house with an intimate sense of privacy; this sunken patio cannot be easily overlooked.

◄ ROOM AT THE TOP
Although the two level areas are equal in size, the lowest would feel confined if filled with furniture; sited in the more open spot at the top, the patio enjoys views across the whole garden.

AN EDIBLE PATIO GARDEN

ALTHOUGH THE TRADITIONAL PATIO GARDEN tends to be purely ornamental, especially in terms of plant material, there is no reason why an equally attractive feature cannot be made using more functional plants – fruit, salads, herbs, and vegetables. The geometric layout of this design, with axes at 45° to the house, creates an opportunity to grow edible crops in a non-traditional way. Posts, wires, trellis, and a pergola provide support for sweet peas and beans and hanging baskets hold alpine strawberries and tumbling tomatoes. Boundary and house walls support fan-trained and cordon fruits, an apple espalier forms an effective screen, and a variety of pots are used to grow strawberries and herbs.

Exposed aggregate flags form patio surface and all ground-level beds are edged in terracotta rope-twist edging tiles

A bed of raspberry canes forms a living screen; the canes are supported on posts and wires using the uprights of the two flanking arches as the terminal points of attachment

Archway is used to support melons and gourds

Raised bed in terracotta-coloured brick for 'Pink Fir Apple' potatoes, carrots, and parsnips

Cordon apples trained on post and wire framework form a screen to enclose patio area and are underplanted with parsley

Herbs in pots include rosemary, sage, thyme, and marjoram

Rhubarb in permanent bed of its own

Sweet peas on trellis for cut flowers

Strawberry tower in sunny position

Gooseberry bush between beds of leafy salads; endives, lettuces, 'Lollo Rosso', and cut-and-come-again salad leaves

Fan-trained pear on wall

N

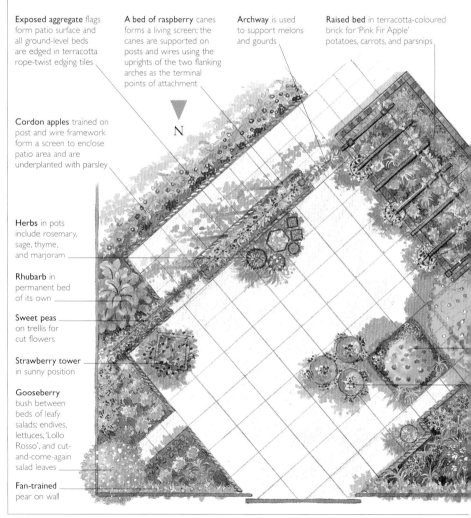

DESIGN BRIEF

- To design a patio that exploits its limited space to grow a range of attractive and good-value edible crops, including culinary herbs, in containers, raised beds and open ground.
- To use both fruit trees and hard landscaping to provide structure to the design.
- To include a water-recycling feature, such as tanks to collect rainwater as run-off from house roof.

Pergola supports climbing French beans and scarlet runner beans

Hanging baskets contain tumbling tomatoes and alpine strawberries

Small crab apple tree, *Malus* 'John Downie', provides fruit for jellies and preserves

Columnar apple tree, *Malus* 'Ballerina'

Pots for peppers and aubergines

Warm, sunny bed with onions, outdoor tomatoes, and herb, bronze fennel

Water tanks collect rainwater run-off from house roof via downspout

A POTTED FEAST

It makes sense to exploit the warm, sunny, sheltered conditions on a patio to grow your own superbly flavoured fruit and vegetables. Many herbs, salads, and vegetables can be grown in pots, provided they are kept well-fed and watered, and this is a really productive way of growing cut-and-come-again crops, like corn salad or endive, perhaps with red lettuce or golden purslane for contrast.

◀ IN THE OPEN
In this neat, formal potager, climbing beans (on pyramids) are interplanted with lettuces of different types that are sown in succession and harvested throughout the summer months.

▼ PEPPER POTS
Sweet peppers and aubergines thrive in pots of good compost in a warm, sunny spot on a patio and their colourful, glossy fruits are attractive, vitamin-rich, and very tasty.

AN URBAN JUNGLE

THE IDEA OF AN URBAN COURTYARD as a haven for wildlife – as well as for its owner – is very contemporary. This design is appropriately informal and full of bold, yet easily managed planting, with great emphasis on encouraging and observing wildlife. There is a range of pollen-, seed- and berry-bearing plants, a fish-free pond for aquatic insects and amphibians, and plenty of cover for birds, butterflies, and insects. The surrounding walls are covered with trellis, fixed away from the wall surface to provide nesting spaces and refuge. In keeping with the mood of the garden, the hard materials are all low-key and sympathetic.

Trellis for climbing plants is fixed away from wall to provide refuge and nesting space for birds; plants include clematis, passion flowers, *Akebia quinata*, and ivy (*Hedera helix*), a late food source for beneficial insects

Grey-leaved *Buddleja fallowiana* has spires of lavender blue flowers in late summer to attract butterflies

Bird nesting boxes sited on trellis in shade

Dwarf willow, *Salix hastata* 'Wehrhahnii', has early spring catkins; a food source for emerging bumble bees

Secluded bench for observation of wildlife

Still water is preferred by most aquatic creatures; pond is stocked with submerged oxygenating plants and waterlily pads provide shade and shelter for frogs, toads and tadpoles

Old railway sleepers form "stepping stones" through a crushed bark path laid on geotextile membrane

Pool has a shallow end bordered by a gently sloping pebble beach to allow easy access for amphibians and a bathing area for birds; boulders provide cool shade and shelter

Dense growth of *Hydrangea petiolaris* on wall provides shady nesting site for birds

DESIGN BRIEF

- To design a courtyard in informal style with a jungle-like abundance of planting that is easy to keep in check.
- To include visually attractive food and shelter plants for birds and insects.
- An area of still water is needed for most aquatic creatures.
- To include a secluded seating area as an observation post.
- To include a bird feeding station and nest boxes.

Holly tree, Ilex aquifolium 'J.C. Van Tol', is self-fertile and bears bright red berries in winter

Purple, nectar-rich flowers of Salvia nemorosa provide food for bees and butterflies from midsummer to autumn

Grasses and bamboos, astilbes, and Alchemilla mollis provide cover for amphibians

Bird table is positioned so that it can also be seen from indoors

Old, mellow red bricks laid in herringbone pattern

Berry-bearing Cotoneaster horizontalis and Pyracantha 'Orange Glow' trained on wall

PLANTING TO ATTRACT WILDLIFE

Even a city garden can be full of wildlife if planted with suitably attractive plants. As well as obvious food sources, like berries and seed-bearing plants for birds and nectar-rich flowers for insects, wildlife needs plants for shelter and sites for nesting and refuge. A water source for amphibians, like frogs, newts, and toads, must have safe, shallow access surrounded by sheltering vegetation.

BUTTERFLY BUSH
Most buddlejas that flower in late summer, like this Buddleja davidii 'Royal Red', *provide an extremely rich source of nectar that butterflies find irresistible.*

WHERE THE BEE SUCKS
Trumpet-shaped flowers, like those of late-summer-flowering Hibiscus syriacus 'Red Heart', *are adapted to invite pollination by butterflies and bees.*

AUTUMN NECTAR
Autumn-flowering sedums, like 'Autumn Joy', *are covered by nectar-seeking butterflies, bees and hoverflies; many of the last are prey for insect-eating birds.*

CATMINTS
All catmints, like this Nepeta sibirica, *belong to the dead-nettle family, most of which bear flowers that are alive with the hum of bees in summer.*

BASIC DESIGN TECHNIQUES

SURVEY AND PREPARATION

B EFORE YOU BEGIN CREATING a design based on your wish list, you will need to carry out a basic, thorough, and accurate survey of your plot and draw it up on paper. You can have fun experimenting with the layout of shapes and spaces, until you find one that pleases the eye. But a pretty layout alone may not fulfil your brief successfully – it must take account of a range of other considerations, both practical and aesthetic, if it is to become a functional design.

TAKING AN OVERVIEW

Hand-in-hand with a survey of obvious features of your garden – boundaries, trees, drain covers and the location of utilities – there are other factors that will affect your design. Areas of sun and shade, dry and damp, are not static; they vary through the day and seasons. Choose a windy day to locate draughty areas. Check for any hollows that may be potential frost pockets. A soil assessment and pH check will tell you what plants are likely to thrive there and if improvements need to be made.

Views out of, and into, your garden may affect where and whether you choose to put up a screen. Look at local stone or building materials and choose materials with similar colours and textures to blend in with them.

LIGHT AND SHADE
When choosing the site and extent of a shade-giving pergola, think about the way light falls and shade changes throughout the day. If, for example, you intend to use it to relax beneath after work, it may be best set at an angle to the setting sun, to avoid the direct glare of low, evening light.

◀ FROM A DISTANCE *Zig-zag panels lead to a sun deck with good views across the garden.*

MEASURING UP

To MEASURE UP YOUR SITE accurately and draw your plan to scale may appear time-consuming, but it is essential to ensure that your design works and can be transferred easily to the ground. You will need to make a base survey plan (*p.53*) to take into account the practical and aesthetic virtues and limitations of the site; a plan of your design on paper (*p.54*) and a setting out plan (*p.55*) to transfer the plan to the ground.

IN GOOD ORDER

To measure up, you will need paper, a pencil, a clipboard, and a 30m (100ft) measuring tape, with a fold-over end that can be hooked onto fixed points. Make a well-spaced, freehand sketch of the garden, including the house, outbuildings, and boundaries to make the rough template that you will annotate with measurements.

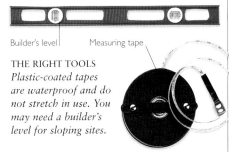

Builder's level   Measuring tape

THE RIGHT TOOLS
*Plastic-coated tapes
are waterproof and do
not stretch in use. You
may need a builder's
level for sloping sites.*

TAKING MEASUREMENTS

The starting point of your survey *must* be a fixed point and, in most cases, this will be the wall of the house. Mark in the house wall dimensions, including the exact position of doors and windows. Then measure and mark in all boundaries, first

fixing the corner points (*see* Fixing a Point, *p.51*). With house and boundaries in place, measure and mark onto the plan all other features, like trees and drain covers. As far as possible, measure to the centre of trees and shrubs and also show their spread.

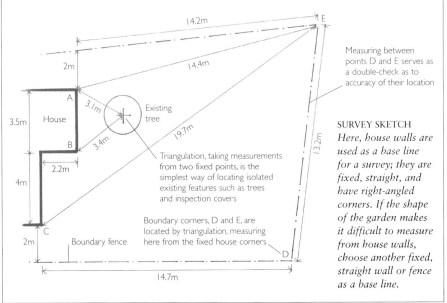

Measuring between
points D and E serves as
a double-check as to
accuracy of their location

SURVEY SKETCH
*Here, house walls are
used as a base line
for a survey; they are
fixed, straight, and
have right-angled
corners. If the shape
of the garden makes
it difficult to measure
from house walls,
choose another fixed,
straight wall or fence
as a base line.*

Triangulation, taking measurements
from two fixed points, is the
simplest way of locating isolated
existing features such as trees
and inspection covers

Boundary corners, D and E, are
located by triangulation, measuring
here from the fixed house corners

FIXING A POINT

The technique known as triangulation is the basis of all survey work. It locates a point simply and accurately by "tying in" the point with two measurements from either end of a fixed baseline of known length. The triangle thus formed is of fixed and precise dimensions and can be accurately plotted on paper using a scale ruler and a pair of compasses.

You will use your sketch plan as the source for measurements that you will transfer to paper when drawing up your survey, design and setting out plans *(pp.53, 54, 55)*. Make sure that every feature that you mark on your sketch has two accurate measurements from two fixed points – one from either end of the fixed base line, which, in this case, is the house wall.

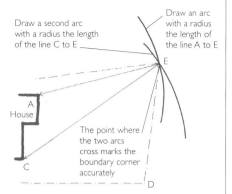

Draw a second arc with a radius the length of the line C to E

Draw an arc with a radius the length of the line A to E

A
House

The point where the two arcs cross marks the boundary corner accurately

DRAWING A BOUNDARY CORNER ON PLAN
Using compasses, draw two arcs, using the measurements from each corner of the house as radii (here, A–E and C–E). The point where the two arcs cross marks the boundary corner.

DEALING WITH SLOPES

Very gentle slopes can usually be accommodated in most gardens without having to resort to making serious changes in level and undergoing major earthworks. Steeply sloping sites, however, may prove impossible to use for a patio without terracing. Large volumes of soil and water exert huge pressures and any slope needing retaining walls higher than 65cm (26in) must have deep foundations and be reinforced. Building regulations are likely to demand professional construction.

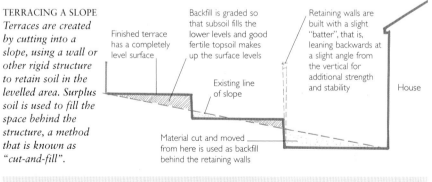

TERRACING A SLOPE
Terraces are created by cutting into a slope, using a wall or other rigid structure to retain soil in the levelled area. Surplus soil is used to fill the space behind the structure, a method that is known as "cut-and-fill".

Finished terrace has a completely level surface

Backfill is graded so that subsoil fills the lower levels and good fertile topsoil makes up the surface levels

Existing line of slope

Retaining walls are built with a slight "batter", that is, leaning backwards at a slight angle from the vertical for additional strength and stability

House

Material cut and moved from here is used as backfill behind the retaining walls

CALLING IN THE PROFESSIONALS

• Seek the advice of your local building or planning control officers on the requirements for structural safety of any proposed terracing.
• Personal recommendation is the best way of finding a reliable builder. Garden centres or builder's merchants may also have contacts.

• Ask to see samples of completed work; obtain and compare competitive quotations and check that insurance-backed guarantees are offered.
• Draw up a written contract agreeing the nature of the work, proposed timescale, and terms of payment.

ASSESSING THE SITE

THE SITE ASSESSMENT AIMS TO survey all the factors that will enhance – or impose limitations – on the final design of your patio or courtyard. They are marked on a base survey plan as a preliminary to designing, to help ensure that nothing is overlooked. Clearly, the zone immediately around the house is most likely to be affected by utilities, so survey this area with extra care. In a new house, the contractor may be able to supply plans of services.

PRACTICAL CONSIDERATIONS

Locate all underground utilities, such as electric, gas, water mains and drains, and feed pipes from external oil supplies. This is critical in order to avoid damaging them, to ensure that they do not coincide with sunken features, like ponds, and to avoid making them inaccessible later. Lift inspection covers to reveal the depth of drains; they usually run in straight lines with access points at junctions. Electronic detectors can be hired to locate live electric cables. Gas mains are less easily detected, but usually enter the house above ground level at a point that is quite obvious.

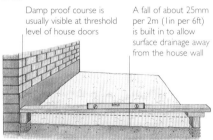

Damp proof course is usually visible at threshold level of house doors

A fall of about 25mm per 2m (1in per 6ft) is built in to allow surface drainage away from the house wall

DAMP COURSES AND DRAINAGE SLOPES
A surface against a house wall must be 15cm (6in) below the damp proof course – usually visible as a black plastic line in a mortar joint.

AESTHETIC CONSIDERATIONS

Views out of the garden may affect your design. Locate those worth preserving, or any that need screening, and determine whether they are visible from the whole garden, or from a single spot. Consider local building materials – stone, flint, or brick, and note any that lend a theme or sympathetic link to the built environment.

CALLING IN THE COUNTRY
The "borrowed" landscape is an old idea that stands the test of time – mature plantings have been left in place to frame the view.

IN SYMPATHETIC HARMONY
Here, planters, furnishing, and paving lend a perfectly unified Period style – in keeping with the aged, mellow brick wall.

MAKING A BASE SURVEY

A base survey is a garden plan drawn from the measurement survey (*see* Drawing up Your Plan, *p. 54*) and annotated with factors that will influence your final design. Recording physical features, such as boundaries, trees, and drains, is obviously vital. Equally important, however, are less tangible factors. Which parts of the garden are sunny or shady and at what times of year, will influence the site of a sitting out area. You may need to filter the effects of a wind tunnel, which may occur regardless of the direction of the prevailing wind. A frost pocket is an unsuitable site for a pond and planting there is restricted to very hardy plants. Soil type will also determine your plant choices – azaleas and rhododendrons, for example, need acid soil.

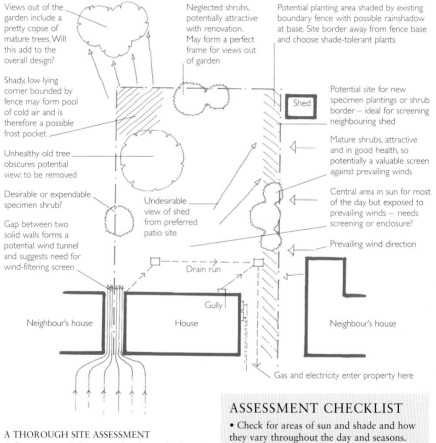

Views out of the garden include a pretty copse of mature trees. Will this add to the overall design?

Neglected shrubs, potentially attractive with renovation. May form a perfect frame for views out of garden

Potential planting area shaded by existing boundary fence with possible rainshadow at base. Site border away from fence base and choose shade-tolerant plants

Shady, low-lying corner bounded by fence may form pool of cold air and is therefore a possible frost pocket

Potential site for new specimen plantings or shrub border – ideal for screening neighbouring shed

Shed

Mature shrubs, attractive and in good health, so potentially a valuable screen against prevailing winds

Unhealthy old tree obscures potential view: to be removed

Desirable or expendable specimen shrub?

Undesirable view of shed from preferred patio site

Central area in sun for most of the day but exposed to prevailing winds – needs screening or enclosure?

Gap between two solid walls forms a potential wind tunnel and suggests need for wind-filtering screen

Prevailing wind direction

Drain run

Gully

Neighbour's house

House

Neighbour's house

Gas and electricity enter property here

A THOROUGH SITE ASSESSMENT

A base survey helps to make clear which areas of the garden are most suited to the various items on your wish list. It also highlights areas where conditions need to be changed. Some annotations may take the form of queries – which of the existing plants are to be retained and why, for example.

ASSESSMENT CHECKLIST

• Check for areas of sun and shade and how they vary throughout the day and seasons.

• Locate any low-lying areas that may form frost pockets.

• Identify potential wind-tunnel effects and the direction of the prevailing wind.

• Check on soil type – acid or alkaline, heavy clay or light sand; in need of improvement?

DESIGNING AND SETTING OUT

A PLAN OF YOUR GARDEN is essential for your base survey (*p.53*), for drawing up your design and setting it out on the ground to begin the practical work. For most small gardens, a scale of 2cm to 1m on the ground (1:50) is usually most convenient. Take the two largest measurements (width and length) and check that they fit on the paper at your chosen scale. If they don't, reduce the scale to 1cm to 1 metre (1:100) or join two or more sheets of paper together.

DRAWING UP YOUR PLAN

Taking the measured dimensions, use a pencil to scale them up onto graph paper, or plain paper using a scale rule. When you are happy that you have pencilled them all in, ink-in permanent features like house walls, boundaries and drain covers. This forms the base survey plan. When drawing up your design, overlay the base plan with tracing paper, copying only the relevant information to avoid clutter. Alternatively, make several photocopies and draw your ideas directly onto them, to give two or three designs that you can lay side by side for comparison.

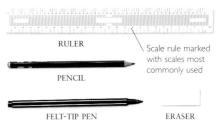

RULER

Scale rule marked with scales most commonly used

PENCIL

FELT-TIP PEN

ERASER

BASIC DRAWING TOOLS
A scale ruler is useful if you decide to draw up on plain paper and a felt tip pen for inking in the position of features you know will not change like boundaries and house walls.

Using graph paper is the simplest way of drawing up your plan. Here, each large square represents one metre, and each small square within it represents 0.1m or 10cm; the scale is 1:100.

A PLAN ON PAPER
At this scale, do not clutter up your drawing with detailed information, like varieties of plants or details of brickwork. It is not essential at this stage. Concentrate on the basic ground shapes of paving, beds, water features, and the position of key plants such as small trees and large, specimen shrubs.

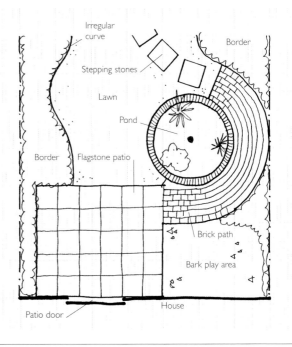

Irregular curve

Border

Stepping stones

Lawn

Pond

Border

Flagstone patio

Brick path

Bark play area

Patio door

House

USEFUL DRAWING TOOLS

Unless you get bitten by the garden-designing bug, you will not want to splash out on a full range of drafting instruments, but it is worth buying a set square and a pair of compasses to draw up your design. A set square is invaluable when creating true right angles, in a formal design, for example. It is also useful in marking off dimensions on your setting out plan, which need to be at right angles to the base line. Try the simple exercise of drawing a circle freehand and the value of a pair of compasses quickly becomes apparent.

USING A SET SQUARE
Use a set square to draw right angles and diagonals. The angles of the other two corners measure 45°.

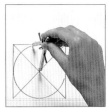

USING COMPASSES
A pair of compasses is essential for circles – it is almost impossible to draw accurate circles freehand.

TRANSFERRING THE DESIGN TO THE GROUND

Using your setting out plan, clearly marked with all the dimensions needed, mark out the positions of the various elements on the ground. Use canes, stakes, or string for straight lines, and sand, or a proprietary marker, for curves (*p.56*). Ensure that marked points are at right angles to the fixed base line (*p.57*).

Once you have the basic shapes in front of you, walk around to ensure that you are satisfied with path widths, space for chairs and tables, and access to various parts of the garden. Use long canes to mark out the positions of screens or trees, then do a final check that they actually line up with the object you wish to hide.

SETTING OUT PLAN
A simple outline plan of your design is used to mark off all the relevant dimensions. Measurements can can be scaled off with a scale ruler, or by counting the graph paper squares. Mark them on the plan at right angles from a fixed base line, such as the boundary fence or house wall.

Boundary fence is a fixed line from which border margins are measured out. Measure curves at widest and narrowest points and several points in-between

Check patio corners with a builder's square and, as a check, confirm that diagonals are equal

For circles (here, the proposed pond) the dimensions include both the radius and the distance of the centre point from the boundary, measured at a right angle to the boundary

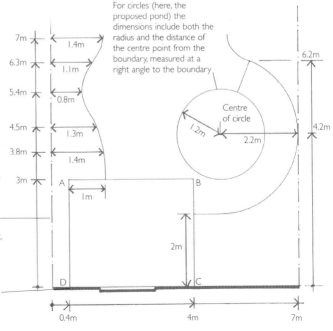

MAKING CURVES AND CIRCLES

You can create circles and curves on the ground quite simply by using what is, in effect, a giant pair of compasses. Knock a peg into the ground at the centre of the circle and loop a string of the desired radius over it. Tie a pointed cane vertically to the other end of the string. Keeping the string taut, inscribe the circle into the soil. To create adjoining curves, use several centre pegs and string lengths of varying radii.

CURVES FROM CIRCLES
Every curve is part of the arc of a circle – the wider the curve, the larger the circle it is part of. You can make a sweeping, sinuous curve by joining up the arcs of several circles.

SWEET CURVES

Broad, sweeping curves are easier on the eye than tight, narrow ones, which give a restless, fussy effect. Broad curves are more practical to construct and, at the lawn edge, simpler to clip or mow around.

Pointed cane inscribes circle

Peg

Peg

Peg

String line of required radius is looped over peg and held taut

Peg placed at centre of circles

Point where two circles touch is on the line joining the two centres

MARKING CURVES ON THE GROUND

In some cases, a pointed cane is not an effective means of marking a circle, perhaps because the ground is too hard to mark, or too soft and crumbly to hold the line. You can use sand, or on hard ground, use a proprietary spray paint marker to follow the line.

▶ USING SPIKES
A sharp-pointed spike is useful for inscribing curves directly onto firm ground, but is less suitable for soft earth.

▶ USING SAND
A trickle of pale-coloured sand can be used as a marker on loose, or soft surfaces like cultivated soil.

PRACTICAL CONSIDERATIONS USING CURVES

When designing with curves, consider carefully the hard materials that you will use to create them. Large unit pavers will need cutting to fit a curve and the tighter the curve, the more cutting is involved. Small units are much easier to lay in curves, or you can buy ready-formed curved units.

A SQUARE PEG IN A ROUND HOLE
Short edges of small pavers fit easily into an arc; long edges are aligned with the radii and small discrepancies between the leading and trailing edge are simply filled in with mortar.

Making a Perfect Right Angle

When setting out, you need to form a perfect right angle to plot points accurately from a base line, or to form square edges on free-standing features, such as a formal pool. Elementary geometry provides the key. Any triangle with sides in the ratio of 3:4:5 (for example, 90:120:150cm or 3:4:5ft) has a right angle opposite its longest side.

You can buy a builder's square, or make a wooden triangle (roofing battens are ideal); the sides can be any convenient length as long as they are in the correct ratio.

Improvise a right-angled triangle using any odd pieces of straight, flat wood, mitred at the corners

The angle opposite the longest side is a perfect right angle, i.e. 90°

SQUARE AND TRUE
The 3:4:5 triangle is a simple but invaluable aid to creating a perfect right angle.

4 units

5 units

3 units

Right Angles on the Ground

Just when think you have grasped the principle of the right-angled triangle, you find that, on the ground, the builder's square is too short to measure any but the shortest distance from the base line. There are several simple techniques, however, that can be used to extend the right angle to the required distance.

For relatively short distances, the easiest technique is to use a spare piece of timber as a straight edge, align it with edge of the builder's square, and measure out along it. For longer distances, peg a length of string or builder's twine firmly on the base line at the corner of the square, aligning it so that it just touches the edge of the square.

▶ EXTENDING A RIGHT ANGLE
To find a point at right angles to a line that is further than the length of your builder's square, lay a straight edge along the side, or a taut line for longer distances.

▼ MARKING OUT A SQUARE
A builder's square can also be used to ensure that the corners of any square or rectangular shape are true right angles; if they are, the diagonals, as measured corner to corner, will also be equal.

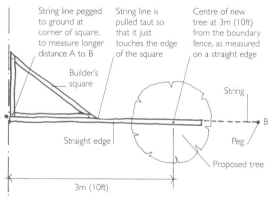

String line pegged to ground at corner of square, to measure longer distance A to B

String line is pulled taut so that it just touches the edge of the square

Centre of new tree at 3m (10ft) from the boundary fence, as measured on a straight edge

Builder's square

String

A

B

Straight edge

Peg

Proposed tree

3m (10ft)

TAPE IT OUT

In some situations, a straight edge is too unwieldy. You will need a helper for this. Take a measuring tape and hold 3m of it firmly along the base line. Fold the tape to form a triangle with the next side 4m long and the last 5m long. Gently pull the sides of the triangle taut and you have formed a 3:4:5 triangle, with a right angle on the base line.

CHOOSING MATERIALS

T HE CHOICE OF MATERIAL FOR PATHS and paving, and how it is laid, will be governed by how the paving will be used, the desired appearance and cost. As a rule, paving for heavy use needs to be rigid for strength and durability and must be laid on a solid base. Hard paving may be made of stone, brick, or concrete or, alternatively, of hard-wearing timber in the form of decking. Lightly or infrequently used areas may be made from loose materials (see *pp.60–61*).

LARGE-UNIT PAVERS

Natural stone flags are relatively expensive compared to other materials, but are very attractive, especially as they age. Square or rectangular flags are available in a range of sizes and may have a smooth finish, or a "riven" finish with lots of uneven texture. Concrete flags come in many colours, sizes, and finishes. Some are very modern, with crisp, sharp edges, while others are made with cast, natural stone aggregate. These give a good imitation of the real thing, yet are more economical and often easier to lay than the genuine article.

ESTIMATING QUANTITIES

• A reputable builder's merchant will be happy to advise on the quantities of paving you need, but will need to know the exact dimensions of the project in hand. To calculate regularly shaped areas, simply multiply the length by the width.

• To calculate irregular areas, draw out the area on graph paper, at a scale of one square per sq.m (or use the plan that you prepared earlier, *see p.54*). Count all of the complete squares and any more than one-third full. This gives a fair approximation of area.

◀ NATURAL STONE
The size variation of stone flags gives an attractive pattern, but demands skill and forethought in matching up.

▶ RECONSTITUTED STONE
Cast stone flags of uniform size are easy to lay. With age, it can be hard to distinguish them from the real thing.

LAYING FIXED PAVING

In areas of heavy use, hard materials, such as flagstones, must be laid on a firm base if they are to remain level and stable. Preparing the base and laying the flags is hard physical labour and can be quite time-consuming. Make a realistic assessment of your skills and available time and, if necessary, consider using a professional.

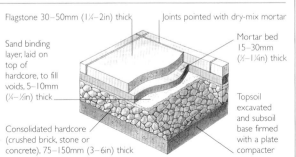

Flagstone 30–50mm (1¼–2in) thick

Sand binding layer, laid on top of hardcore, to fill voids, 5–10mm (¼–½in) thick

Consolidated hardcore (crushed brick, stone or concrete), 75–150mm (3–6in) thick

Joints pointed with dry-mix mortar

Mortar bed 15–30mm (½–1¼in) thick

Topsoil excavated and subsoil base firmed with a plate compacter

SMALL-UNIT PAVING

Bricks make excellent pavers, provided that they are frost-proof. Some hard, well-burnt house bricks and engineering bricks are suitable for paving, but many other, softer bricks are not – they flake and shatter in frost if laid on the ground. Pavers come in many shapes and sizes, and give an even surface suitable for a patio or path. Setts are slightly rounded and best used for paths and edging, rather than for placing tables and chairs on. Cobbles are similar in size to setts, but are even more rounded and are best restricted to edgings and infills that receive little or no foot traffic.

◄ BRICK PAVERS
Brick pavers are formed from traditional, moulded clay or cast concrete; some are made to look like old bricks.

► SETTS
Setts are small, exceptionally hard-wearing cubes of stone, usually granite or sandstone. Although expensive, they last, quite literally, for centuries.

CUTTING PAVERS

When cutting pavers, be sure to wear safety goggles to protect your eyes. Lay the paver on a firm, flat surface, and score a groove along the intended line of cut using a bolster chisel and club hammer. (If you place the paver on a length of narrow timber and align the groove with the timber edge, it will split cleanly.) Put the bolster chisel blade in the groove and tap the other end with a club hammer until the paver splits.

Place chisel blade in groove and strike with club hammer to break paver

Use bolster chisel blade to score groove along line of cut

TIMBER DECKING

Wood in the form of decking, is a very sympathetic material. The priority when constructing decking is to choose a durable hardwood (from a sustainably managed source) or a pressure-treated softwood. Specially made decking boards have a reeded finish to provide a non-slip surface. Decking is assembled on concrete block foundations to keep it clear of the ground and allow ventilation beneath.

WOOD DECKING
Decking boards should be fixed in place with a 5–7mm (¼in) space between each slat to allow for expansion. Timber will swell when wet and, without an expansion joint, will buckle and may lift from its moorings.

CARE OF WOOD

• Wooden surfaces need regular maintenance. Check them annually and replace any damaged timber.

• Scour surfaces regularly with a stiff brush and sand to control algal growth. If using chemical cleaners, make sure that they are safe to use with plants.

LOOSE MATERIALS

Loose materials can be laid in a more flexible, fluid way than fixed paving and are especially useful for curved forms. They fall into two broad groups – plant-derived materials such as crushed bark, wood chips, and cocoa shells, or harder, mineral-based ones, like gravel, stone chippings, or slate.

Gravels or pebbles, dredged from ancient lakes or riverbeds, are smooth in texture. Locally quarried types have a colour range that blends well with other local materials. Grades less than 6mm (¼in) will "walk" onto surrounds on the soles of shoes, while any larger than 12mm (½in) are difficult to walk on. Stone chippings, derived from crushed rock, have an angular texture, so choose smaller grades for easy walking.

WHAT MATERIAL WHERE?

• Wood products, such as crushed bark or woodchips, give terrific textural harmonies in a wild or woodland-style design. They also make a good surface for children's play areas.
• Crushed sea shells, a waste product of the shellfish industry, look perfectly at home in a seaside garden.
• Broken slate is an ideal material for creating striking visual effects, perhaps laid to imitate a dry stream bed, or to form a colour contrast within a sweep of gravel.
• Scatter groups of variably sized cobbles randomly within slates or gravels to gain interesting textural contrasts. You might also use them as direction markers, or to deter from areas that should not be walked on.

SLATE CHIPPINGS
The cool, grey-blue of slate contrasts well with mellow brickwork and the warmer tones of gravel.

GRAVEL
Gravels show colour variation in every batch, but this means that they tone perfectly with local stone and brick.

CRUSHED GLASS
Processed to give rounded edges, crushed glass gives a good walking surface. It comes in a range of colours.

USING GEOTEXTILE MEMBRANE

Laying loose materials on a geotextile membrane helps suppress weed growth. It also extends the life of the materials by preventing them from being incorporated into the soil beneath, especially important if the material is walked on frequently. Plants can be introduced by slitting the membrane and planting through the hole.

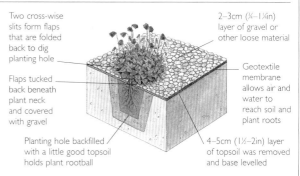

Two cross-wise slits form flaps that are folded back to dig planting hole

Flaps tucked back beneath plant neck and covered with gravel

Planting hole backfilled with a little good topsoil holds plant rootball

2–3cm (¾–1¼in) layer of gravel or other loose material

Geotextile membrane allows air and water to reach soil and plant roots

4–5cm (1½–2in) layer of topsoil was removed and base levelled

MIXED MEDIA

Mixing paving media provides lots of opportunities to introduce variety and contrast and to imprint your individual stamp on a design. You could, for example, make a patio from stone flags and omit one or two as planting pockets to be topped off with loose gravel. Alternatively, you could complement the principal paving material with smaller elements, like terracotta tiles, to form a pattern of contrasting colour. Alternatively, use a series of flags in gravel, or perhaps log sections in mulched bark areas, to make attractive stepping stones that also act as directional markers.

COBBLED SQUARE
Water-worn cobbles edged with clay tiles, all pressed firmly into mortar base, mark the junction of two paths.

CRAZY MIXTURE
Clay tiles form a decorative, starburst pattern within crazy paving to lend additional interest to a patio surface.

DECORATIVE CONCRETE
A cast concrete disc, imprinted with a leaf when wet, makes a pretty stepping stone through loose gravel.

EDGING MATERIALS

One of the drawbacks of loose materials is that they tend to get kicked onto adjacent planting beds, or onto lawns, where they may then be thrown dangerously into the air by mower blades. They need some form of slightly raised edge as a boundary to prevent this. Edging can be as simple as a timber gravel board held in place with pegs, or a row of durable paving bricks bedded in mortar. Specially designed terracotta edging tiles are also available with scalloped or barley twist tops.

KEEPING IT ALL IN PLACE

• A row of water-worn cobbles mortared in place makes a suitable edging for pea gravel, or, perhaps to emphasize a maritime theme, crushed sea shells. Cobbles also look good with crushed slate.

• Timber boards, perhaps in the form of reclaimed sleepers, look perfectly at home as a retaining edge for woodchips, crushed bark, or cocoa shells. All other timbers for outdoor use must be pressure-treated to ensure a long, useful life.

• Bricks, clay pavers, and granite setts set in mortar give a firm, crisp edge that suits designs of a more formal style.

DECKING EDGE
Edging bricks form a "mowing strip" at the deck's edge to prevent damage to the timbers by mower blades.

GRAVEL EDGING
Gravel is held neatly in place by a curved row of durable bricks that are mortared firmly in place.

FURNISHING THE DESIGN

D URABLE FURNITURE IS AN ESSENTIAL PART of outdoor living and should be considered as part of the design process. The quantity and size of furniture depends on how you will use the space – regular dining, for example, will need a table and chairs and perhaps a shade umbrella, but if you simply want to sit in the sun, a couple of loungers may fit the bill. Having decided on its function, choose a material and style of furniture that sits well with the rest of your garden.

METAL AND PLASTIC FURNITURE

Metal furniture is, by and large, hard-wearing, long-lasting, and need not break the bank. A wide range of styles is available. To suit a more traditional garden style, you might select ornate wrought-iron furniture, or, for a more modern, geometric layout, chrome and toughened, child-proof glass. Most wrought-iron work is epoxy-coated or painted to keep it free of rust, while aluminium is, by its very nature, rust-resistant and low-maintenance.

Plastics, among the least costly of outdoor furniture, are usually resistant to UV light to a degree. Even the best eventually becomes brittle with time and exposure, however, so to preserve it, think about how and where you might store it when not in use.

MODERN CHAIR
*Polished aluminium is
lightweight and does
not rust and may
come ready lacquered
to preserve the shine.*

WOODEN FURNITURE

Available in styles both traditional and modern, wood brings its own natural warmth and beauty to a design, especially if finished with oils or varnish. Most wood also takes stains and paints well, so can be coloured to suit your theme. Although wood is sometimes expensive, its cost merely reflects its durability and longevity.

SUSTAINABLE SOURCES

Tropical hardwoods, like teak and iroko, are exceptionally durable outdoors. They may be very costly, but last a lifetime. There are, however, environmental concerns with regard to over-extraction of tropical timbers, so do check that the furniture is certified as being from sustainably managed forests.

HARDWOOD TABLE AND CHAIRS
*Most hardwoods mellow gracefully to tones
of blonde and ash-grey, but if you want it to
remain pristine, treat it regularly with a
penetrating oil or wood preservative.*

BARBECUE AND ENTERTAINING AREAS

Eating outside may involve a barbecue and, if this is on the wish list, should be thought about at the planning stage. The major decision is whether to have a fixed feature, or to use one of the many mobile variations available that can be moved round to suit prevailing conditions. Fixed barbecues can look good and function efficiently, but don't take account of changing wind direction, which may cause problems with smoke. Don't forget to take into account the need for a wipe-clean surface for raw ingredients and the other accoutrements needed for cooking outdoors.

HAUTE CUISINE
A permanent barbecue can mesh perfectly with a design, if you use matching materials that tie in with surrounding walls and paving.

LIGHTING YOUR PATIO

The favourable microclimate of patios and courtyards, coupled with a convenient location next to the house, makes a good case for lighting them so they can be used beyond daylight hours into the evening. Outdoor lighting falls into two broad types.

First, there is lighting for convenience and safety, especially if there are changes in levels. Secondary lighting can be used to highlight focal points, or to create special effects, such as pencil spots or uplighters that focus on feature plants.

AMBIENT GLOW
The soft glow from a light source with a translucent shade gives glare-free lighting for outdoor dining at night. Additional low-tech lighting in the form of candles or lanterns may be all that is needed to enhance the mood.

SAFETY FIRST

• General lighting can be permanently installed and controlled from an indoor switch, or a weatherproof, outdoor switch.
• Lighting powered from a socket outlet should not be of the 230 volt type, but should operate via an isolating transformer at less than 50 volts. These readily available DIY systems offer flexibility as well as safety.

LOOKING AFTER PATIO FURNITURE

During the season, most furniture needs an occasional wash down, especially in damp or dusty climates. Give metals and plastics a more thorough clean before storage, with a proprietary cleaner, or soap and water. Check the care label for wooden items; some woods simply need oiling, others may need a more specific preservative treatment.

Warm, soapy water and soft-bristled brush is satisfactory, low-tech cleaner for metals

REGULAR WASHING
Use soap or a dilute solution of household bleach to remove algae from plastics.

Caring for the Plants

Many patios and courtyards are located in hot, sunny locations that dry out rapidly. Coupled with this, the drainage fall of a patio mean that planting areas on its "uphill" sides are deprived of a proportion of rainfall. So you need to make provisions to provide adequate moisture for plants to thrive. In open ground, incorporating organic matter prior to planting aids soil water retention. For containers and raised beds, you need to take special steps.

Feeding and Watering

All plants need adequate water and nutrients to grow well and, if soil volumes are limited, as in containers, they rely on the gardener to supply these needs. Keep the growing mix evenly moist and never allow it to dry out completely. Liquid feeds act fast and are easy to use. Use a high-nitrogen feed for foliage plants and a high-potash formulation for flowering ones.

A FINITE RESOURCE

Container plants rely on a limited amount of growing medium to supply nutrients and water. Loam-based mediums have good moisture- and nutrient-retaining qualities and their weight lends stability to containers. If using a lighter, soilless mix, add slow-release fertilizer granules and water-retaining gel.

Using Irrigation Systems

Irrigation systems provide water by overhead sprinklers, by surface or sub-surface capillary action via porous pipes, or by spot watering by means of drip lines. They can be controlled manually, turning a tap on or off as needed, or by a timeswitch that can be set to come on at pre-selected times and frequencies.

Dripper is placed at base of each plant

Filter fitted to water supply tap

Supply pipe to drippers

MICRO-IRRIGATION
Drip lines supply water directly to the root zone. Some can be run directly from a tank that collects rainwater.

Conserving Water

Water conservation is a necessity for environmental reasons and, in many areas, there may be restrictions on watering during the hot summer months, when plants need it most. So conserving water is essential. Mulching the soil surface with loose materials, like gravel or chipped bark, reduces moisture loss from the soil surface by evaporation and keeps plant roots cool, resulting in less stress to the plants. Mulches also suppress weeds that compete for water and nutrients.

WATER-RETAINING GRANULES

◀ RETAINING WATER
Water-retaining gels increase the moisture-holding capacity of growing mediums in containers. Simply mix dry granules into the potting medium and water them in thoroughly.

◀ USING MULCHES
Mulches can also have an aesthetic value in acting as a background to the plantings. Gravel is the perfect choice for bringing plants of strong outline into high relief.

RAISED BEDS

Raised beds fall somewhere in-between open soil and containers in terms of supplying plants with water and nutrients. They hold larger volumes of soil than containers and therefore retain moisture for longer, particularly if the insides are lined with plastic, or coated with a water sealant. They can be filled with a specially prepared growing mix to suit the plants you want to grow – perhaps a gritty mix for succulents that need free drainage, or an acidic mix for lime-hating plants, like azaleas.

PLANTS FOR RAISED BEDS

Aurinia saxatilis (Gold dust) Evergreen perennial with grey-green leaves and masses of golden yellow flowers in late spring and early summer. Excellent for trailing over the edges.
Origanum 'Kent Beauty' Trailing, aromatic, semi-evergreen perennial with heads of rose-pink and mauve flowers in summer.
Lithodora diffusa 'Heavenly Blue' Trailing, evergreen shrub with intense blue flowers in spring and early summer. Needs acid soil.
Rosmarinus officinalis 'Prostratus' A trailing variant of common rosemary with masses of blue flowers in mid-spring and early summer. Enjoys the enhanced drainage of a raised bed.

FILLING A RAISED BED
Add a layer of rubble before filling the bed with good quality topsoil. A depth of 45cm (18in) allows a wide range of plants to thrive.

CONTAINERS ON THE PATIO

Containers can dry out very rapidly and may need daily watering, especially in hot, dry weather. Drip-line irrigation is very effective, especially for large numbers of pots. Otherwise, be sure to site pots within easy reach of a tap, and use a watering can. Try to avoid siting containers in spots that are particularly hot or windy.

IT'S IN THE BOX
Plants that make a long-term contribution to your patio, like this close-clipped box, need a container of adequate dimensions. If they dry out, you risk spoiling years of effort.

Clean lines of classic wooden planter provide perfect setting for pyramid of box (*Buxus sempervirens*)

GOOD CONTAINER SHRUBS

Acer palmatum (Japanese maple) A compact, deciduous tree with lobed leaves that have brilliant autumn colour. Site out of winds.
Citrus × *meyeri* (Meyer's lemon) A compact, evergreen tree with sweetly scented flowers followed by small lemons. Move to a frost-free greenhouse for the winter in cold areas.
Ilex crenata (Box-leaved holly) A compact, evergreen shrub with glossy, oval, dark green leaves. May produce white or yellow berries from its inconspicuous flowers.
Laurus nobilis (Bay laurel) Aromatic, evergreen shrub with clusters of tiny, yellow-green flowers in spring. Can be clipped as a standard or pyramid. It is also used as a culinary herb.
Myrtus communis (Common myrtle) Delightfully aromatic evergreen with fragrant, ivory-white flowers in late summer. Ideal for scenting a sitting-out area. Can be trimmed to a ball or pyramid. In cold areas, bring into a greenhouse, or onto a verandah, for winter.
Rosa (Roses) Choose one of the many dwarf, floribundas or miniature roses for blooms all summer long.

PLANTS FOR PATIOS AND COURTYARDS

THE FOLLOWING PLANTS have been grouped to correspond with the special conditions of different patios and courtyards – first those that are suitable for hot, sunny spots, and then ones for cool, shady sites. Certain plants have also been selected for their fragrance, which is ideal for enclosed spaces, and others for their year-round value or exceptionally long period of interest.

◨ *Prefers full sun* ▨ *Prefers partial shade* ▩ *Tolerates full shade* ◊ *Prefers well-drained soil* ◔ *Prefers moist soil* ◆ *Prefers wet soil* ❋❋❋ *Fully hardy (down to –15°C/5°F)* ❋❋ *Frost-hardy (down to –5°C/23°F)* ♔ *RHS Award of Garden Merit*

SUN- AND DROUGHT-TOLERANT PLANTS

NOT ONLY DO THE FOLLOWING plants tolerate hot, dry conditions – they positively revel in them and often flower more freely in these conditions. They represent a tiny proportion of the plants that enjoy dry heat, but note how many of them have fleshy, white, or grey-hairy leaves. This feature is an excellent indicator that a plant will thrive in a hot spot.

Artemisia 'Powis Castle' ♔
Woody-stemmed, non-flowering evergreen, up to 60cm (24in) tall, by 75cm (30in) across. Finely cut, silver-grey leaves form a dense mound that is an ideal foil for flowering or coloured foliage plants. For best foliage, cut back in spring and trim again in midsummer to keep neat.
◨ ◊ ❋❋

Caryopteris × *clandonensis*
Graceful, deciduous, shrubby perennial, with aromatic, grey-green, silver-hairy leaves and dense clusters of rich blue flowers from late summer to autumn. Cut back in spring for good foliage and flowers. It reaches 1m (3ft) tall.
◨ ◊ ❋❋

Cistus × *cyprius* ♔ (Rock rose, Sun rose)
A bushy, evergreen shrub, to 1.5m (5ft) tall, with dark green leaves and large, white, paper-thin flowers, with a basal crimson blotch, from early to midsummer. An ideal framework shrub that can also be wall-trained. Trim after flowering to keep bushy.
◨ ◊ ❋❋

CISTUS × *CYPRIUS*

◁ FROM THE GROUND UP *Good-value plants at every level provide interest for most of the year.*

Cytisus × *praecox* 'Allgold' ♀
(Broom)
Deciduous shrub with dense
masses of narrow, rush-like
stems with tiny green leaves,
forming an arching mound to
1.5m (5ft) tall by as much
across. From mid- to late
spring it is covered with
pungently scented, rich golden
yellow, pea-like flowers.
Tolerant of very poor, dry
soils, it makes excellent tall
ground cover on steeply
sloping banks.
◫ ◊ ❁❁❁

Eryngium giganteum ♀
(Miss Willmott's ghost)
A short-lived, rosette-forming
perennial forming a crown of
spiky, silvery blue leaves.
During summer, it bears
branched heads of long-
persistent, steel-blue flowers
with a ruff of silver bracts
beneath, reaching 90cm (3ft)
tall. Although it is short-lived,
it self-seeds readily, so leave
some seedlings undisturbed as
future replacements. This
makes a striking feature
plant, looking particularly
good at twilight.
◫ ◊ ❁❁❁

ERYNGIUM GIGANTEUM

EUPHORBIA CHARACIAS

Euphorbia characias
An upright, evergreen shrub
forming a bushy mound to
1.2m (4ft) tall and wide.
Narrow, blue-green leaves
radiate from thick, succulent
stems, topped by a head of
tiny flowers surrounded by
large, yellow-green bracts,
black-purple at the base. An
excellent architectural plant,
especially grown as a specimen
through gravel or stones.
◫ ◊ ❁❁❁

Festuca glauca ♀ (Blue
fescue, Grey fescue)
An evergreen, clump-forming
grass forming a neat, spiky
mound of stiff blue-green
leaves, to 30cm (1ft) high.
The slender stems are topped
by minute, buff-coloured
flowers in late spring and
early summer. It makes an
excellent colour foil for other
flowering plants and is superb
as a low, informal edging,
particularly in dry gravel
beds. Divide and replant every
three years to maintain good
foliage colour. The cultivar
'Blaufuchs' ♀, syn. 'Blue Fox',
has brighter blue leaves.
◫ ◊ ❁❁❁

HELIANTHEMUM 'FIRE DRAGON' ♀

Helianthemum (Rock rose,
Sun rose)
Small, spreading, evergreen
shrubs, about 20cm (8in) tall
and 60cm (24in) across. The
dense, wiry stems are clothed
in tiny, grey-green leaves and
the whole plant is covered
with a succession of papery,
brightly coloured flowers in
late spring and early summer.
Striking in a hot spot and
excellent as ground cover, or
for trailing over dry walls.
Trim immediately after
flowering to keep bushy.
◫ ◊ ❁❁❁

Iris, Tall bearded
The tall bearded irises grow
to 70cm (28in) or more in
height and produce fans of
sword-shaped, grey-green
leaves from thick, fleshy
surface rhizomes. In mid-
spring to early summer, they
bear spikes of large flowers in
shades of white, yellow,
apricot, pink, and blue and
often in lovely colour
combinations. All make good
accent plants, flowering
profusely – and earlier – at
the base of a warm wall.
◫ ◊ ❁❁❁

Osteospermum jucundum ♥
A neat, low-growing, spreading perennial with narrow, grey-green leaves bearing a long succession of daisy-like, rich mauve-pink flowers throughout summer. They close in dull weather to reveal deep coppery pink undersides. It makes excellent ground cover, particularly on dry, sunny banks. It is very tolerant of poor, dry soils and thrives in seaside gardens, even within reach of sea spray. It reaches 10–50cm (4–20in) high and will form a mat up to 90cm (3ft) across.
🔲 ◊ ❋❋❋

OSTEOSPERMUM JUCUNDUM

Sedum spectabile 'Brilliant' ♥
(Ice plant)
A robust perennial with stout stems, to 45cm (18in) tall, bearing whorls of fleshy, pale grey-green leaves. In late summer and autumn, it produces broad, flat heads of many tiny, deep rose-pink flowers that remain attractive even as they die and fade to brown. An excellent plant for attracting bees and butterflies in to the garden.
🔲 ◊ ❋❋❋

Sempervivum tectorum ♥
(Common houseleek)
A succulent, evergreen, ground-hugging perennial forming neat rosettes of fleshy, bristle-tipped, blue-green leaves that are often flushed maroon or red-purple. During summer, it produces upright stems topped by heads of tiny red-purple flowers. It will form a dense mat, 15cm (6in) high by 50cm (20in) across. The houseleeks need minimal soil and moisture and so are excellent for growing in gravel and wall or paving crevices, or in broad, shallow troughs or other containers.
🔲 ◊ ❋❋❋

SEDUM SPECTABILE 'BRILLIANT'

Stipa gigantea ♥ (Giant feather grass, Golden oats)
A perennial, evergreen or semi-evergreen grass, forming dense, arching clumps of narrow, mid-green leaves. In mid- to late summer, it produces tall spikes of tiny golden flowers on slender stems that shimmer in the slightest breeze, creating a hazy effect that is especially effective against a dark background. It makes a dramatic focal point among lower level plantings, and can reach up to 2.5m (8ft) in height, by 1.2m (4ft) across.
🔲 ◊ ❋❋❋

MORE CHOICES FOR HOT SPOTS

Cordyline australis ♥ Small, palm-like tree with arching leaves and heads of white, spiky flowers in summer.
Eremophila glabra Low-growing shrub with grey-green leaves and green, yellow or red flowers throughout summer.
Euonymus fortunei Low-growing, evergreen shrubs. In many cultivars, the dark green leaves are heavily variegated with gold or white (*see p.70*).
Juniperus squamata 'Blue Star' ♥ Compact, rounded evergreen conifer with silvery blue leaves.
Onopordum acanthium Giant, thistle-like biennial with white-hairy, spiky leaves and tall spikes of purple flowers in summer.
Phlomis fruticosa ♥ Medium-sized, evergreen shrub with aromatic, grey-green leaves and whorls of yellow flowers in summer.
Pinus mugo Small, evergreen conifer with dark green, needle-like leaves.
Yucca gloriosa ♥ Tall, spiky, rosette-forming perennial with huge spikes of white flowers in summer.

SHADE-TOLERANT PLANTS

To THE NEW GARDENER, shady spots can seem to be a problem, but this is far from the case. Many beautiful plants actually prefer shade and, in the cool, sheltered shade of a courtyard, will look good for much longer – in both foliage and flower – than if subjected to bleaching sunlight and buffeting winds.

Aucuba japonica 'Crotonifolia' ♀

A tough, evergreen shrub with glossy, green leaves, splashed and mottled with gold. A fine choice for brightening a dark corner, tolerating a wide range of conditions and soils. It reaches 2m (6ft) tall by 2m (6ft) across, but if it outgrows its position, can be cut back hard in spring.

Dicentra spectabilis 'Alba' ♀ (Dutchman's breeches)

A perennial with finely cut, pale green leaves and arching stems bearing heart-shaped white flowers from early to midsummer. It dies back in late summer, so plant with autumn-flowering bulbs, such as colchicums, to follow on.

HELLEBORUS × BALLARDIAE 'DECEMBER DAWN'

Digitalis purpurea (Common foxglove)

Rosette-forming biennial or short-lived perennial with mounds of soft, mid-green leaves and upright spikes, to 2m (6ft) tall, of hooded, white-spotted, purple flowers in early summer. A long-flowering feature plant for sun or shade. It self-seeds readily and naturalizes easily.

Euonymus fortunei 'Emerald 'n' Gold' ♀

A very tough, evergreen shrub with glossy green, gold-margined leaves that are often pink-flushed in winter. An excellent highlight plant for any soil in sun or shade. Usually to 90cm (3ft) tall, but will climb much higher if grown against a wall or fence.

Helleborus (Hellebore)

A genus of herbaceous and evergreen perennials with leathery, divided leaves and usually nodding, cup-shaped flowers in a range of subtle colours, from pale green to white, mauve, purple, and slate-grey. Depending on species, they flower for very long periods between mid-winter to mid-spring, reaching 25–60cm tall (10–24in). They are excellent cut flowers for winter arrangements.

HOSTA FORTUNEI VAR. *ALBOPICTA*

Hosta (Plantain lily)

Hostas are clump-forming herbaceous perennials grown mainly for their beautiful foliage, but also for the spikes of scented, pale-lavender midsummer flowers. They range from tiny cultivars, like 'Blue Moon', at 10cm (4in) tall, to large-leaved ones, such as *H. fortunei* var. *albopicta* ♀, to 1m (3ft) tall by as much across. Some, such as *H. sieboldiana* var. *elegans* ♀ have bold, deeply puckered leaves of rich blue-green, forming a mound 1m (3ft) tall. Large-leaved hostas are excellent ground-cover plants for shade, or for sun if the soil is reliably moist. Many look extremely elegant when grown in containers. The flowers are good for cutting.

HYDRANGEA MACROPHYLLA
'LANARTH WHITE'

Hydrangea macrophylla 'Lanarth White' ♥

A deciduous shrub, to 1.5m (5ft) tall, with fresh green leaves and heads of white, "lacecap" flowers in mid- to late summer. An elegant specimen plant for a cool, shady corner, it can also be grown in large containers. The flowers are good for cutting and drying. Many cultivars of *H. macrophylla* are available. Some, the "hortensias", have rounded flowerheads. Except in white-flowered types, soil influences the flower colour; they are blue on acidic soils and pink on alkaline ones.

▣ – ▨ ◊ ✾✾✾

Lamium maculatum 'Album' (Dead nettle)

A spreading perennial, to 15cm (6in) tall, with pale green, silver-zoned leaves and a succession of white flowers from late spring to early summer. It is excellent for ground cover, even on poor soils. Trim back to 5–10cm (2–4in) after flowering.

▣ – ▨ ◊–◊ ✾✾✾

Polygonatum × hybridum ♥ (Common Solomon's seal)

An herbaceous perennial with slender, gently arching stems clad with horizontally held, mid-green leaves. In late spring, it bears pendulous, green-tipped white flowers. This elegant plant is at its best in cool, humus-rich soil that remains reliably moist.

▣ – ▨ ◊ ✾✾✾

Polystichum setiferum 'Pulcherrimum' ♥

This variant of the soft shield fern produces arching, silky fronds with long, gracefully upswept segments, which emerge from a central crown. It has a striking architectural form and makes good ground cover, reaching 60–80cm (24–32in) tall. Remove the dead, old fronds before the new ones unfurl. Like many ferns, it is at its best in humus-rich soils that do not dry out. As a group, the ferns are shade-lovers *par excellence* and there are many more that will thrive in the shelter of a cool courtyard.

▣ – ▨ ◊ ✾✾✾

POLYSTICHUM SETIFERUM
'PULCHERRIMUM'

RHODODENDRON
YAKUSHIMANUM

Rhododendron yakushimanum

One of the loveliest of the rhododendrons, forming a neat, evergreen mound of glossy, dark green foliage covered with trusses of white or pale pink flowers in mid-spring, which open from rose-pink buds. The new leaves have thick buff-brown hairs beneath. It grows slowly to 2m (6ft) and can be grown in containers of ericaceous (acid) compost in areas where the soil is alkaline or limy.

▣ – ▨ ◊ ✾✾✾

Saxifraga fortunei ♥

An herbaceous or semi-evergreen perennial forming neat, 30cm (12in) tall mounds of deeply lobed, dark green leaves that are red beneath. In late summer or autumn, it bears delicate spikes of white flowers. An excellent, late-flowering feature plant for ground cover. Such conditions also suit the mat-forming mossy saxifrages, like 'Apple Blossom' with pink-flushed white flowers in late spring.

▨ – ▨ ◊ ✾✾✾

Fragrant Plants for Patios

SCENT CAN BE EPHEMERAL in the open garden, whisked away by the slightest breeze, but in the still air of a courtyard, or the confined space of a patio, the perfume that emanates from plants is greatly enhanced. The plants described here will add a many-layered dimension of fragrance to your designs.

Erysimum × cheiri 'Harpur Crewe' ♥ (Wallflower)
A shrubby, evergreen perennial, to 30cm (12in) tall, with light green leaves and tight heads of small, strongly scented, deep yellow flowers from early spring to summer. Trim after flowering to keep dense and bushy.
◙ ◊ ❋❋❋

Jasminum officinale ♥ (Common jasmine)
A vigorous, deciduous or semi-evergreen climber with dark green leaves on twining stems. The heavily scented white flowers are borne from summer to early autumn. It reaches 12m (40ft) in height and is an excellent climber for clothing pergolas, pillars, arches, and gazebos.
◙ ◊ ❋❋

INDISPENSABLES

Dianthus The modern pinks are compact, grey-leaved perennials with clove-scented flowers all summer. Ideal with roses.
Lilium Many lilies have intensely fragrant flowers flowers and are ideal for borders, especially with roses. They look especially elegant in large containers on patios or in courtyards.

Lathyrus odoratus ♥ (Sweet pea)
Climbing annual with greyish green leaves. Scented flowers in a wide range of colours – white, cream, deep and pale pink, mauve, or blue, are borne continuously from early to midsummer. Equally good in open ground and in pots, trained on trellis or wigwams. Reaches 2m (6ft) tall.
◙ ◊ ❋❋❋

Lavandula angustifolia (Lavender)
Evergreen, aromatic, grey-leaved shrub, 60cm (2ft) tall, with spikes of blue-purple flowers in mid- to late summer. Can be used as a low hedge, in a border, in pots, and for planting in gravel. Lavenders with pink or white flowers, or a more compact habit are also available.
◙ ◊ ❋❋❋

Nicotiana sylvestris ♥ (Flowering tobacco)
A biennial or short-lived perennial with branching stems bearing heads of sweetly fragrant, tubular white flowers over long periods in summer.
◙ ◊ ❋❋❋

Philadelphus (Mock orange, Syringa)
Deciduous shrubs with light green leaves and masses of white flowers in early and midsummer, with a scent of orange blossom. Cultivars 'Manteau d'Hermine' ♥, 'Belle Etoile' ♥, 'Avalanche' and 'Girandole' all reach 1.5m (5ft) or less and are excellent choices for confined spaces. Most tolerate light shade, but flower best in sun.
◙ ◊ ❋❋❋

LAVANDULA ANGUSTIFOLIA 'TWICKEL PURPLE' ♥

PHILADELPHUS 'MANTEAU D' HERMINE'

PHLOX PANICULATA 'HAMPTON COURT'

Phlox paniculata
(Perennial phlox)
Herbaceous perennials, to 90–120cm (3–4ft) tall, with fresh green foliage and upright stems bearing large heads of very fragrant, white, pink, red, or pale to deep purple flowers in mid- to late summer or early autumn.
⊡ ◊ ❀❀❀

Rosa
The rose is one of the world's favourite fragrant flowers and there are thousands to choose from, with scents ranging from sweet and fruity to spicy or musky. Most modern climbers, modern shrub, large-flowered and cluster-flowered roses flower repeatedly in summer. Old Garden roses have fabulous scent but bloom mainly in one glorious, midsummer flush. 'Aloha' is a modern climber with glossy, dark green foliage and sweetly scented, rose-pink flowers tinted deep pink on the reverse. It reaches 3m (10ft) on a wall and blooms nearly all through summer.
⊡ ◊ ❀❀❀

Rosmarinus officinalis
(Rosemary)
Aromatic, evergreen shrub with dark green leaves and spikes of tiny flowers in various shades of blue, from mid- to late spring, or earlier if protected by a warm wall. Excellent as a low informal hedge, in a gravel garden and invaluable for culinary use; plant some by the barbecue. Cut back by up to a third after flowering to keep bushy.
⊡ ◊ ❀❀

Syringa vulgaris 'Decaisne'
(Lilac)
A small tree with heart-shaped leaves and spikes of many tiny, fragrant, purplish blue flowers in late spring or early summer. At 2.5m (8ft) tall, it is much more compact than many lilacs and is an excellent choice for smaller gardens. Even smaller is the bushy *S. meyeri* 'Palibin' ♀, to 1.5m (5ft) tall. It has heavily scented, lavender-pink flowers in late spring. Lilacs tolerate most soils, preferring slightly alkaline (limy) ones.
⊡ ◊ ❀❀❀

ROSA 'ALOHA'

VIBURNUM × BURKWOODII 'ANNE RUSSELL'

Viburnum × burkwoodii 'Anne Russell' ♀
A compact, deciduous or semi-evergreen shrub with glossy, dark green leaves and rounded heads of heavily fragrant, pink-flushed, white flowers that open in late spring from deep pink buds. Excellent as a framework shrub and as a backdrop to smaller, flowering and foliage plants. Trim lightly after flowering to keep in shape.
⊡–⊡ ◊ ❀❀❀

Wisteria sinensis ♀
(Chinese wisteria)
Vigorous twining climber with pale green leaves divided into oval leaflets. It bears long chains of fragrant, pea-like, lilac-blue flowers in late spring and early summer. *W. sinensis* 'Alba' ♀ has white flowers and is a spectacular climber for a pergola or high wall, reaching 9m (28ft) or more, but can be pruned and trained to keep it at a relatively modest size. It can even be trained as a standard and grown in a container.
⊡–⊡ ◊ ❀❀❀

PLANTS WITH A LONG-LASTING SHOW

A LL PLANTS MUST WORK HARD to earn their place in a small space. The plants in the catalogue do just that, either by providing exceptionally long seasons of bloom or foliage interest, or by putting on a performance for more than one season, perhaps flowers in spring and fruits or brilliant colour in autumn.

Abelia × *grandiflora* ♥
Evergreen or semi-evergreen shrub, to 3m (10ft) tall, with glossy, dark green leaves. It bears a succession of tubular, pink-flushed, white flowers over a long period from midsummer to late autumn. A good framework shrub that can also be loosely trained against a warm wall.
◫ ◊ ❄❄

Acanthus spinosus ♥
(Bear's breeches)
Herbaceous perennial with large, very glossy, dark green leaves that are deeply cut and spiny. Tall, bold spikes of hooded, white and purple flowers, 1.5m (5ft) tall, appear from early to late summer. A striking feature plant both in leaf and flower. The flowers can also be cut and dried for arrangements.
◫ – ◪ ◊ ❄❄❄

MORE CHOICES

Alchemilla mollis ♥
Ground-cover perennial with rounded, pale green leaves and lime-green flowers all summer.
Berberis thunbergii ♥
Deciduous, spiny shrub with bright green leaves that turn red in autumn. Sprays of yellow spring flowers are followed by rounded, red fruits.

AGAPANTHUS 'BLUE GIANT'

Achillea 'Moonshine' ♥
An aromatic, herbaceous perennial forming mounds of soft, deeply cut, silvery green foliage. From early summer to early autumn, produces long white-woolly stems topped by flat heads of soft yellow flowers. An excellent foil for darker-leaved plants and good for cutting and drying. It reaches 60cm (2ft) in height.
◫ ◊ ❄❄❄

Actinidia kolomikta ♥
Deciduous climber, to 4m (12ft) tall, with twining stems clad with heart-shaped leaves, the first emerging green, tinged purple and successive ones becoming splashed with pink and white at the tips. An excellent feature plant for wall, trellis, or pergola.
◫ ◊ ❄❄❄

Agapanthus 'Blue Giant'
(African blue lily)
Clump-forming perennial with strap-shaped leaves. Slender stems, to 1.2m (4ft) tall, bear large, rounded heads of dark blue flowers in mid- to late summer. Striking in a sunny border or a large container.
◫ ◊ ❄❄❄

Anemone × *hybrida*
(Japanese anemone)
Spreading perennial, to 1.5m (5ft) tall, with softly hairy leaves and golden-centred, pale pink flowers for many weeks in late summer and autumn. The flowers of its cultivars range from white to deep pink. The white blooms of 'Honorine Jobert' ♥ glow in shade, or at twilight. All make good ground cover.
◫ – ◪ ◊ ❄❄❄

ANEMONE × HYBRIDA
'HONORINE JOBERT'

ANTHEMIS PUNCTATA SUBSP.
CUPANIANA

Anthemis punctata subsp. cupaniana ♀

Mat-forming perennial, to 30cm (12in) tall, with soft, finely cut, silver-grey leaves that look good throughout spring and summer. Large, white, golden-centred daisies are borne over several weeks, from early summer. Excellent as low ground cover, as edging, or trailing over the wall of a raised bed. The silver leaves are a perfect foil for brightly coloured flowers.
◻ ◊ ❄❄❄

Carex oshimensis 'Evergold' ♀

An evergreen grass forming clumps of narrow, dark green, arching leaves boldly striped with bright, creamy yellow. Slender spikes of small, buff and brown flowers are borne in late spring, followed by delicate seedheads. A neat foliage plant, to 30cm (12in) tall, that retains its colour through most of the year. Suitable for border edges, it also looks good in containers, either alone as a specimen, or in a mixed planting.
◻ – ◼ ◊ ❄❄❄

Ceratostigma plumbaginoides ♀

Spreading, semi-evergreen, woody-based perennial, to 45cm (18in) tall, with rounded, bristly leaves that become red-tinted in autumn. Spikes of brilliant, rich blue flowers appear from late summer to autumn, the last flush at the same time as the leaves colour. An excellent plant for ground cover and at the front of a border.
◻ ◊ ❄❄❄

Cornus kousa var. chinensis ♀ (Flowering dogwood)

A small tree, to 7m (22ft) tall, with dark green leaves that turn rich red in autumn. In early summer, it bears tiny green flowers surrounded by large, creamy white, petal-like bracts, that turn white then pink. 'China Girl' has olive-green leaves that turn fiery red in autumn and is free-flowering, even when young; 'Stella' has pointed, starry bracts. They prefer neutral to acid soil and dislike shallow soils over chalk.
◻ – ◼ ◊ ❄❄❄

CAREX OSHIMENSIS
'EVERGOLD'

COTINUS 'GRACE'

Cotinus 'Grace' ♀ (Smoke bush)

Bushy shrub or small tree, to 6m (20ft) tall, with soft, rounded purple leaves on dark-tipped stems, turning rich shades of red in autumn. In late summer, bears fluffy heads of tiny, purple-pink flowers that create a misty haze over the foliage. An excellent highlight feature that also forms a fine contrast with grey-leaved shrubs.
◻ – ◼ ◊ ❄❄❄

Dicentra 'Stuart Boothman' ♀

Spreading perennial, with deeply cut, soft grey-green foliage that forms dense, ground-covering mounds. It is covered with a prolonged succession of pendulous, heart-shaped, deep pink flowers from mid- to late spring until late summer, and sometimes beyond. An excellent edging plant that thrives in sun or light shade; it is also good for planting beneath deciduous, flowering shrubs of open habit, for example, *Cornus kousa* var. *chinensis* or *Hibiscus syriacus*.
◻ – ◼ ◊ ❄❄❄

FUCHSIA MAGELLANICA

Fuchsia magellanica
(Lady's eardrops)
A upright shrub, reaching 3m (10ft) tall in mild regions; in cold areas, it reaches 1.5m (5ft) and dies back to the ground in winter, like a perennial. It has smooth, mid-green leaves and produces a succession of slender, pendent, crimson and purple flowers throughout summer into autumn. In cold regions, mulch the base in winter and cut back dead stems to just above ground level in spring.
◫ – ◪ ◊ ❀❀

Hydrangea 'Preziosa' ♥
Upright, deciduous shrub, to 1.5m (5ft) tall, with dark-tipped stems bearing glossy, mid-green leaves that flush purple in autumn. It produces large, rounded, long-lasting heads of flowers, white at first, turning rose-pink and then deep crimson, or blue or mauve, on acid soil. Flowers appear in midsummer and last until late autumn. A beautiful feature shrub for late-season interest in light shade, or in full sun on moisture-retentive soils.
◫ – ◪ ◊ ❀❀

Hypericum 'Hidcote' ♥
Dense, evergreen or semi-evergreen shrub, to 1.2m (4ft) tall, with dark green leaves. It bears a long succession of cup-shaped, rich golden yellow flowers from early to midsummer until mid- to late autumn. A shapely bush that thrives in virtually any well-drained soil.
◫ ◊ ❀❀❀

Malus × zumi 'Golden Hornet' ♥
This ornamental crab apple is a slender, deciduous tree, to 10m (30ft) tall, with dark green leaves and a profusion of white flowers in spring. The small, golden crab apples that follow are borne in great profusion and often persist until long after leaf fall. There are many lovely ornamental crabs – most are small trees. All have blossom in spring, from wine-red in 'Lemoinei', pink in 'Magdeburgensis' to white in 'Katherine' ♥; they produce crab apples in shades of red, gold, or purple-red.
◫ ◊ ❀❀❀

HYPERICUM 'HIDCOTE'

PHYGELIUS AEQUALIS 'YELLOW TRUMPET'

Phygelius aequalis 'Yellow Trumpet' ♥
Small, upright, suckering shrub, to 1m (3ft) in height, with narrow, glossy, dark green leaves. It bears a profusion of exotic, trumpet-shaped, fuchsia-like flowers in soft, creamy yellow, through the summer into autumn. It flowers most freely in a sunny, sheltered corner, in moist, humus-enriched soil.
◫ ◊ – ◊ ❀❀

Potentilla fruticosa 'Elizabeth' ♥
Bushy, deciduous shrub, to 1m (3ft) tall, with tiny, grey-green leaves on twiggy stems. It bears masses of saucer-shaped, canary-yellow flowers throughout summer. It thrives in virtually any well-drained soil. Trim lightly in spring to keep neat and compact and to induce better flowering. There are many to choose from, with flowers ranging from white ('Abbotswood' ♥) through shades of yellow, orange ('Tangerine' ♥), to pink and scarlet.
◫ ◊ ❀❀❀

Pyracantha atalantioides
(Firethorn)
Upright, evergreen shrub, to
6m (20ft) tall, with glossy,
dark green leaves on shiny,
spiny stems. In late spring, it
bears clusters of small white
flowers followed by a
profusion of long-lasting,
bright, orange-red berries. An
excellent framework shrub,
especially if trained against a
wall. The berries of this, and
many other pyracanthas, are
attractive to birds, so they are
ideal for a wildlife garden.
▣ ◊ ✿✿

Rudbeckia fulgida var.
sullivantii 'Goldsturm' ♀
(Black-eyed Susan)
Mound-forming, herbaceous
perennial, to 60cm (2ft) tall,
with pointed, dark green
leaves. From mid- to late
summer until autumn, it
produces bright yellow,
daisy-like flowers that have
cone-shaped, dark brown
centres. A superb feature
perennial for any good,
moisture-retentive soil.
Flowers are good for cutting.
▣ ◊ ✿✿✿

Spiraea japonica
'Goldflame' ♀
Deciduous shrub, to 75cm
(30in) tall, with leaves that
emerge bronze-red, then
turn bright golden yellow
flushed red before finally
becoming pale green. It also
has good autumn colour. In
early to midsummer, it bears
heads of bowl-shaped, deep
pink flowers. The best foliage
is had by cutting back hard
in early spring.
▣ ◊ ✿✿✿

Viburnum opulus
'Compactum' ♀ (Guelder rose)
Bushy, deciduous shrub, to
1.5m (5ft) tall, with maple-
like, dark-green leaves that
turn gold and red in autumn.
In late spring and early
summer, it bears flattened
heads of white flowers,
followed, in autumn, by a
crop of glossy, bright red
berries that persist after leaf
fall. An excellent feature and
framework shrub that is
smaller than *V. opulus*. It
thrives in any well-drained
soil in sun, or light shade.
▣ ◊ ✿✿✿

VIOLA CORNUTA

Viola cornuta ♀
(Horned violet)
An evergreen perennial, to
about 7–10cm (3–4in) tall,
with heart-shaped, mid-green
leaves that form a dense,
tufted mound. From spring to
summer, it bears a succession
of small, slightly scented,
pansy-like flowers, with violet
to lilac-blue petals, the lower
ones marked with white. An
excellent edging plant and
suitable for gravel plantings
and troughs.
▣ – ▨ ◊ – ◊ ✿✿✿

Vitis vinifera 'Purpurea' ♀
(Vine)
Deciduous climber, to 7m
(22ft) tall, with large, deeply
lobed, plum-purple leaves
that are grey-hairy when
young. Tiny flowers in early
summer produce bunches of
beautiful, but inedible, purple,
white-bloomed grapes. In
autumn, the leaves colour
brilliantly in shades of red
and purple. A dramatic
climber for a sunny site on a
wall, an arch, or pergola, and
very useful for disguising
unsightly buildings.
▣ – ▨ ◊ ✿✿✿

RUDBECKIA FULGIDA VAR.
SULLIVANTII 'GOLDSTURM'

VIBURNUM OPULUS
'COMPACTUM'

INDEX

ACKNOWLEDGMENTS

Picture Research Anna Grapes
DK Picture Librarian Richard Dabb
Garden plans Designed by the author;
illustrated by Gill Tomblin
Additional illustrations Karen Gavin
Index Hilary Bird
Special photography Trish Gant

Dorling Kindersley would like to thank:
All staff at the RHS, in particular Susanne
Mitchell and Barbara Haynes; Alison Copland
for editorial assistance.

The Royal Horticultural Society
To learn more about the work of the Society,
visit the RHS on the internet at
www.rhs.org.uk. Information offered includes
plant news, horticultural events around the
country, RHS *Plant Finder*, a garden finder,
international plant registers, results of plant
trials, a gardening calendar and monthly
topics of interest, publications and
membership details.

Photography
The publisher would like to thank the following
for their kind permission to reproduce their
photographs:
(key: t=top, c=centre, b=bottom, l=left, r=right,
fj=front jacket, bj=back jacket)

Garden Picture Library: Henk Dijkman 12br;
Tim Griffiths 66; Lamontagne 5bc, 39t, 61bc;
Marie O'Hara 41t; Gary Rogers 35t; Ron
Sutherland 2, 14cl, 15br; 27b, fj and 27t;
Brigitte Thomas 4br, 11cr, 52bl.
Jerry Harpur: 4bl, 4bc, 9tl, 9cr, 16b, 20br, 29t,
37t; Michael Balston fj and 33t; Tom Corruth
and John Furman 48; Sonny Garcia, San
Francisco 6, 11bl; Simon Fraser 5br, 13t, bj and
43t; Marcus Harpur 52br; Keyes Brothers 5bl,
bj and 33b; Chris Rosmini, LA 25t, 37b; Ian
Teh, London 20bl; Tim Du Val, NYC 17tr;
Robert Watson 22, John Wheatman 49br.
Clive Nichols: Jonathan Baillie 21b; Christopher Bradley-Hole 18br; Clare Matthews bj
and 10, 29br; Jane Nichols 45b.